O9-AIC-650

CHICAGO
WHITE SOX
TRIVIA TEASERS

RICHARD PENNINGTON

QUIZ MASTER BOOKS
Madison, Wisconsin

©2008 Richard Pennington

All rights reserved. No part of this publication may be reproduced or transmitted
in any form or by any means, electronic or mechanical, including photocopying
and recording, or by any information storage and retrieval system without
written permission from the publisher.

Library of Congress Control Number: 2008921877
ISBN: 978-1-934553-02-2

Editor: Mark Knickelbine
Designer: Rebecca Finkel
Photos: National Baseball Hall of Fame Library,
Cooperstown, New York

Printed in the United States of America.
13 12 11 10 09 08   6 5 4 3 2 1

Quiz Master Books, a division of Big Earth Publishing
923 Williamson Street • Madison, WI 53703
(800) 258-5830 • www.trailsbooks.com

TABLE OF CONTENTS

Comiskey Park, home of the White Sox from 1910 to 1990.

CHAPTER ONE

THE OLD ROMAN

The origins of the White Sox franchise can be traced to one person: Charles Albert Comiskey, the third of eight children in a family that lived in Chicago. His father, a political boss and alderman, was not thrilled with Charles' affinity for baseball, preferring that he become a business-man or perhaps a plumber. He was sent to a small college in Kansas, where it was hoped he would buckle down. Instead, he met Ted Sullivan, one of the pioneers of organized baseball. Sullivan would start two leagues and manage four teams, and was a great promoter of the game. Comiskey played first base for Sullivan in Milwaukee and Dubuque, and later replaced his mentor as manager of the St. Louis Browns. He led the team to four straight American Association championships, and was also a player/man-ager for the Chicago Pirates of the Players League and the Cincinnati Reds of the National League. Comiskey's career as a player (he took part in 1,390 games, batted .264, and stole 378 bases) and manager (a won-loss record of 839-542) ended in 1894.

Comiskey took a chance that year, leaving the majors to buy the Sioux City Cornhuskers of the Western League, which he promptly moved to St. Paul, Minnesota. For five years, the St. Paul Saints shared the Twin Cities with another Western League club across the river, the Minneapolis Millers. Comiskey packed up and moved the team to Chicago, home of a well-established National League franchise. William Hulbert's team did not adopt the name "Cubs" until 1902; before that, they were the Orphans (sometimes called the Remnants), the Colts, and—originally—the White Stockings. Comiskey decided to revive that old name, and thus the new Chicago White Stockings came into existence. The Cubs, if we may sim-plify by using that name, played at West Side Park, and the newcomers of the American League set up shop a few miles south of there in 1900. The AL would declare itself a major league the next year, although references to the "junior circuit" are still part of baseball's lexicon.

Now, as to the team's name. Sports writers and especially those who composed headlines at the *Chicago Tribune* were soon shortening it to "White Sox," which the team officially adopted in 1903. Baseball historians point to a game in which scorekeeper Christoph Hynes wrote "White Sox" at the top of a scorecard rather than "White Stockings." Comiskey was agreeable, and from then on the name was set.

As owner of the White Sox for more than three decades, Comiskey oversaw the construction in 1910 of a facility that would bear his name, five American League championships, and two World Series triumphs. A notoriously frugal and hard-nosed businessman, the "Old Roman" was quite unpopular with his players, a fact that is widely conceded as having influenced eight of them to throw the 1919 Series.

Where did the White Sox originally play?

They played at South Side Park, of which there were three incarnations all within a few blocks of each other. The first, in the neighborhood of 39th Street and South Wabash Avenue, was the home of a pro team in the Union Association in 1884. It was succeeded by another facility of the same name at 35th Street and South Wentworth Avenue. One tenant of South Side Park II was the Chicago Pirates of the Players League in 1890, and another was the National League team that came to be called the Chicago Cubs in the early 1890s. South Side Park III, the longest-lived venue of that name, was built on 39th Street between South Wentworth Avenue and South Princeton Avenue. Charles Comiskey, owner of the White Stockings, built a wooden grandstand there in 1900, and it was the team's home field for 11 years. The ballpark, which could hold crowds as large as 15,000, was abandoned in the middle of the 1910 season when Comiskey opened a new steel-and-concrete facility that would soon be named after him.

Q What became of South Side Park III after the Sox left?

A Its new tenant was the Chicago American Giants of the recently formed Negro League. Team owner Rube Foster renamed it Schorling's Park in honor of his white business partner, John Schorling, a local saloonkeeper who leased the grounds. The American Giants played at Schorling's Park until 1940 when it was destroyed by fire. Their final 10 seasons would be held at Comiskey Park. The site was turned into public housing and apparently got so polluted that it became a Superfund cleanup project.

Q The Western League, led by President Ban Johnson, was ready to challenge the National League's monopoly. It renamed itself the American League in October 1899, declared independence the next year, and began to sign NL players. How did Comiskey's team do in that first year of the AL's existence?

A Their first game was an exhibition on April 2, 1900, against the University of Illinois, downstate in Champaign. Roy Patterson was the winning pitcher in a 10-9 defeat of the Illini. Against their fellow pros, the White Stockings did quite well, winning the championship with an 82-53 record. Trailing them were the Milwaukee Brewers, Indianapolis Hoosiers, Detroit Tigers, Kansas City Blues, Cleveland Lake Shores (soon to be renamed the Blues and eventually the Indians), Buffalo Bisons, and Minneapolis Millers.

Q The AL had begun calling itself a major league in 1901, but that was in name only as is seen in the NL's refusal to engage the AL in a post-season playoff of any kind—both in 1901 and in 1902. Still, the American League was making serious inroads. No franchise was stronger than the one in Chicago. How did the club do in '01?

A They won the title, finishing four games ahead of Boston (a team that had not yet taken on the name of "Red Sox"). Home attendance was 354,350, the top batter was Fielder Jones (.340), Sam Mertes had 5 home runs, and Clark Griffith (24-7) was the ace of the White Stockings' pitching staff. This dominance did not last, however. They finished fourth in 1902 and seventh in '03 as Boston had the honor of representing the AL in the inaugural World Series.

Q Chicago roughed up the Cleveland Blues' rookie pitcher, Charles Baker, on April 28, 1901. What did they do to the young man?

A The White Stockings got 23 singles off him in a 13-1 victory.

Q What was the usual lineup for the 1901 White Stockings?

A Frank Isbell at first base, Sam Mertes at second, Frank Shugart at shortstop, Fred Hartman at third, Fielder Jones, Dummy Hoy, and Herm McFarland in the outfield, and Billy Sullivan behind the plate. The pitching rotation consisted of Roy Patterson, Clark Griffith, Jack Katoll, and Nixey Callahan.

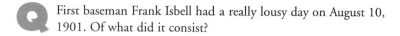

Q First baseman Frank Isbell had a really lousy day on August 10, 1901. Of what did it consist?

A In a game against the Cleveland Blues, he left 11 men on base, setting an American League record in the process. Isbell would, however, lead the league in stolen bases (52) that year.

Q What Wisconsin native was the Sox' primary catcher for more than a decade?

A Billy Sullivan, who had a reputation as a fine catcher but a woeful hitter. Sullivan had a .212 lifetime batting average, making him one of the worst among those with at least 3,000 at-bats. Nevertheless, with Sullivan behind the plate, the ChiSox won a pair of pennants and came close two other times.

Q Sullivan, Chicago's manager in the 1909 season, later had a son on the team. Who was he?

A Billy Sullivan, Jr., whose major league career included stops with the Sox, Reds, Indians, Browns, Tigers, Giants, and Pirates. Primarily an infielder during his years with Chicago (1931–1933), he later moved behind the plate like the old man.

Q This center fielder had been a major leaguer with several teams since 1888, but his only season with Chicago came in 1901 when he batted .294 and led the AL with 86 walks. Name him. Hint: He is considered the most accomplished deaf player in the game's history.

A William Ellsworth "Dummy" Hoy. Some sources credit him with causing the establishment of signals for safe and out calls, although the evidence for this claim is slim. Until 1920, Hoy held the major league record for games in center field (1,726).

Q Some 20,000 fans were on hand for a rare Sunday game on September 8, 1901, when Chicago hosted Boston. Hoy laced a two-run single in the bottom of the ninth for a 4-3 victory. What great pitcher gave up that hit to Hoy?

A Cy Young.

Q Clark Griffith was the Chicago White Stockings' first manager, in 1901 and 1902. Where had he come from?

A Griffith, known as the "Old Fox," was a native of Clear Creek, Missouri. He had pitched in the major leagues since 1891 with the St. Louis Browns, Boston Reds, and Chicago Orphans/Colts (the Cubs' precursors). In his first year at the helm, he won 20 games and the team won the AL title with an 83-53 record.

Q And where did Griffith go after leaving Chicago in 1902?

A He was a baseball lifer, spending no fewer than 64 years in the game. He was also player/manager with the New York Highlanders (soon to become the Yankees; 1903–1908), Cincinnati Reds (1909–1911), and Washington Senators (1912–1914). Griffith continued managing the Senators through the 1920 season, concluding his career from the dugout with a record of 1,491-1,367. Griffith then purchased the Washington club and ran it until his death in 1955. Since he was a man of limited means, Griffith had to be an innovative owner, seeking good ballplayers who were willing to work for low wages. In that role, he signed dozens of mixed-race Cubans and Venezuelans, beginning with outfielder/third baseman Bobby Estallela in the mid-1930s. Thus it is certain that Jackie Robinson was not the first person of African heritage to play major league baseball.

Q Who threw the first no-hitter in franchise history?

A James Joseph "Nixey" Callahan, who did it against the Detroit Tigers on September 20, 1902.

Q It was a rather inelegant game on May 6, 1903, when the White Stockings and Tigers met. What happened?

A Chicago committed 12 errors, and Detroit had six. The Sox made up a two-run deficit in the ninth inning to win, 10-9.

Q Who was the first man to have two stints as manager of the White Stockings?

A Callahan. He held the job (as player/manager) in 1903 and for the first 42 games of 1904, and was back in Chicago from 1912 to 1914. Callahan owned a local semi-pro team that earned the ire of AL President Ban Johnson because many of his players were major leaguers using assumed names. Comiskey paid what was then a sizable $700 fine to have Callahan's suspension rescinded, and he was back with the Sox in 1911. Comiskey appointed him as the club's manager for a second stint in 1912. He moved to the front office after three years and managed the Pittsburgh Pirates in 1916 and 1917.

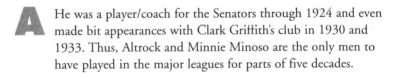

Q Left-handed Nick Altrock started playing major league ball in 1898, won 61 games for the Sox from 1904 to 1906, and was a key figure for the '06 champs. He suffered an arm injury but managed to hang on—for how long?

A He was a player/coach for the Senators through 1924 and even made bit appearances with Clark Griffith's club in 1930 and 1933. Thus, Altrock and Minnie Minoso are the only men to have played in the major leagues for parts of five decades.

Q For what else was Altrock known?

A He was a comedian extraordinaire. While coaching, he often did physical comedy routines (such as a one-man wrestling match) in the third base coach's box to distract and amuse the opposing pitcher. When AL President Ban Johnson heard of it, he came to investigate. Johnson was roaring along with the crowd, but he still told Altrock to quash the funny business.

Q Identify the Sox's manager from 1904 to 1908.

A That was the appropriately named Fielder Jones, who had spent five years playing outfield for the Brooklyn Superbas before joining the Chicago team of the newly formed American League in 1901. He took over as manager for Nixey Callahan in the summer of 1904 and for five years played no fewer than 144 games while handling the team's managing duties. After leaving Chicago, Jones managed the St. Louis Browns for three seasons but with little success.

Q This big, strong pitcher played 13 seasons for the Sox and was at his peak from 1906 to 1912 when he averaged 24 victories per year. Identify him.

A Ed Walsh, who used a dominating spitball throughout his career. The Pennsylvania native, who twice threw more than 400 innings in a season, deserves to be remembered for his 1908 campaign in which he compiled a 40-15 record, completed 42 of 49 games, had 11 shutouts, and struck out 269. Walsh's career ERA (1.82) is the lowest of any player, but this record is not official since the AL did not recognize earned-run average until 1913.

Q Name the left-handed hurler who lost 25 games for the 1903 White Stockings.

A Patrick "Patsy" Flaherty, who gave up 338 hits that year. In 1904, he was sold to the Pittsburgh Pirates for $750 and proceeded to win 19 games for Fred Clarke's club. Flaherty had power for the dead ball era and was occasionally used as a pinch hitter. He once had three hits in a game.

Q The 1903 season was not a good one in team history. The Sox finished 30½ games out of first, and attendance was dropping. Did things pick up?

A They certainly did. Chicago finished in third place in 1904, second in '05, and won the pennant the next year with a 93-58 record. Jones' club was derided as the "hitless wonders" due to their puny batting average of .230. Among the regular players, Frank Isbell was the best at .279, and shortstop George Davis led them with 80 RBIs. They hit a total of seven home runs. What got them by was a fine pitching staff that included Frank Owen, Nick Altrock, Doc White, and Ed Walsh, who won 79 games among them. The '06 Sox pitchers had a combined ERA of 2.13.

Q What other White Sox team would be known as the "hitless wonders"?

A Eddie Stanky's 1967 club, which came close to winning the pennant. They were in first place in the American League for 89 days despite finishing the season with a .225 batting average.

Q Who was on the mound on August 23, 1906, when the Sox won their 19th straight game?

A Roy Patterson, as Chicago beat the Senators by a score of 4-1. He had first come to the attention of Charles Comiskey in 1898 when the St. Paul Saints lost an exhibition game to the Duluth Dukes. He was rewarded with a Saints contract the next year. When the Saints moved to Chicago to become the White Stockings, the young right-hander from St. Croix Falls, Wisconsin, was the team's top pitcher.

Q What honor does Patterson hold in American League history?

A When the AL declared itself a major league in 1901, Chicago chose Patterson to pitch the opening game of that season. On April 24, he became the league's first winning pitcher, defeating the Cleveland Blues, 8-2, as all the day's other games were rained out. Patterson stayed with the Sox through the 1907 season.

Q Who would be their National League foe in the 1906 World Series?

A It was a cross-town matchup with the Chicago Cubs, who had won the most games (116) and had the best winning percentage (.763) in the big leagues since the advent of the 154-game season. The Cubs were heavy favorites.

Q Did the Sox acquit themselves well against this baseball juggernaut?

A Jones' club won it in six games for one of the biggest upsets in World Series history. Game 5 was an entertaining affair that featured 18 hits, 10 walks, 6 errors, 3 wild pitches, 2 hit batters, and 1 steal of home. Walsh won for the second time, with relief help from Doc White. The next day, back at South Side Park, the White Sox battered Mordecai Brown for 7 runs on 8 hits and got another solid pitching performance from White in an 8-3 win that secured the Series.

Q Who was the surprise star of the 1906 World Series for the Sox?

A George Rohe, an unheralded utility infielder. Shortstop George Davis was injured on the eve of the Series, so Rohe was pressed into service at third base, as Lee Tannehill moved to short. In Game 1, he tripled and scored in a 2-1 White Sox victory, and in Game 3 his bases-loaded triple drove in all three of the team's runs. He batted .348 in the six games, although he did commit three of the team's 15 errors. After the final game, Comiskey was heard to say, "Whatever George Rohe may do from now on, he's signed for life with me!" Not really; Rohe was released at the end of the 1908 season.

Q What is the club record for steals in a game?

A The White Sox swiped 11 in a 15-3 defeat of the St. Louis Browns at South Side Park in 1909.

Q What was the Sox' winning share from the '06 Series?

A $1,874 apiece. For the losing Cubs, it was $440. In the South Siders' euphoric clubhouse, Comiskey made what seemed like a generous move, handing a $15,000 check to Jones and telling him to divide it among the players. They soon learned that the money was only for raises the team was due in 1907. Comiskey's deception was a harbinger of his fiscal shenanigans, which would eventually sow the seeds for scandal.

Q Name the Pittsburgh native who led the AL in strikeouts (177) in 1909 and tossed no-hitters against the Tigers in '05 and the A's in '08.

A Frank Smith, who went by the nickname "Piano Mover." This burly right-hander had a problem with alcohol but was a fine pitcher when sober. During the 1908 pennant race, he abandoned the team after feuding with manager Fielder Jones but was persuaded to return. In a widely discussed move, Jones chose to put Doc White on the mound instead of a rested Smith on the last day of the season. The White Sox lost the game—and the pennant— to Detroit.

Q South Side Park, made almost entirely of wood, was not going to be the Sox' home for too long. What did Comiskey do in 1909?

A He hired Zachary T. Davis of the Osborne Engineering Company to design a big, modern, and quite stately new facility at 35th Street and Shields Avenue. With a price tag of $750,000, its original name of White Sox Park soon turned into Comiskey Park, and it would be the team's home for the next 81 seasons. The major leagues' fourth concrete-and-steel stadium, it had room for nearly 29,000 patrons. None were bigger at the time. Comiskey fancied it "the Baseball Palace of the World," and several Chicago sportswriters were only too happy to go along with that. Comiskey Park was christened on July 1, 1910, with a 2-0 loss to the St. Louis Browns.

Q What other famous Chicago sports facility did Davis design four years later?

A Weeghman Park, later renamed Wrigley Field.

Q When was Comiskey Park first expanded?

A Average attendance was just over 9,000 per game in 1926, but Comiskey decided to erect double-decked outfield bleachers. This raised seating capacity to 52,000. Other modifications came in 1938, 1939, 1940, 1942, 1969, and 1981, but it never really got any bigger. The South Side ballpark had pitcher-friendly proportions (362' to the foul poles, 420' down the middle) and remained favorable to defensive teams throughout its history. During that history, more than 6,000 major league games were played.

Q Comiskey Park was the site of the All-Star Game three times. Enumerate them if you can.

A Major league baseball's first All-Star Game, a promotion put on by *Chicago Tribune* sports editor Arch Ward, was held at Comiskey Park in 1933. The AL got a home run from Babe Ruth in defeating the NL; the Americans would win 12 of the first 16 Midsummer Classics. Comiskey Park next hosted the game in 1950, won by the National League in extra innings. The '50 game may be best remembered for Ted Williams colliding with the outfield wall, breaking his elbow, putting him out the rest of the season. The 50th anniversary All-Star Game in 1983 was in Chicago in commemoration of the first one. It was a lopsided win for the AL, highlighted by Fred Lynn's grand slam.

Q Doc White was a White Sox hurler from 1903 to 1913. He won 18 games for the world champion Sox in 1906 and 27 games the next year. What team record does he still hold?

A In 1904, White went 45 straight innings without giving up a run.

Q Who hit the first home run in the history of Comiskey Park?

A The Sox' utility infielder Lee Tannehill did it against the Tigers on August 1, 1910. Tannehill did not hit another one all year long.

Q What publicity stunt did White Sox pitcher Ed Walsh and catcher Billy Sullivan pull off on August 24, 1910?

A From atop the Washington Monument, Walsh dropped 23 balls before Sullivan was able to snare one. The estimated speed of these balls, which fell 555 feet earthward, was 161 feet per second. Remarkable as Sullivan's catch was, it had been done before— by Pop Schriver in 1894 and Gabby Street in 1908.

Q Hugh Duffy was the Sox' manager in 1910 and 1911. What is his well-earned and lasting claim to fame?

A In 1894, as a member of the Boston Beaneaters, Duffy had one of the greatest offensive seasons ever: 18 home runs, 145 RBIs, and a .440 batting average. The latter mark is still the major league record and will be for as long as the game is played.

Q What ambitious barnstorming tour did Callahan help put on between October 1913 and March 1914?

A He organized one in which the White Sox and the New York Giants played each other in exhibitions across the U.S., then moving to Japan, Hong Kong, China, the Philippines, Australia, Egypt (at the base of the Pyramids), Sri Lanka, France, Italy, and the United Kingdom.

Q Why did Comiskey reach down to Peoria of the Triple-I League for a new manager in 1914?

A His legendary cheapness, as much as anything, led him to tab Clarence "Pants" Rowland to take over the club. Rowland had never played, coached, or managed in the majors, so fans and journalists were a bit surprised. In his first year, his Sox finished 93-61, good enough for third place in the AL; the next year, they were second. With Rowland at the helm in 1917, Chicago went 100-54 and beat the New York Giants in the World Series. Getting fired by Comiskey after a sixth-place finish in 1918 was a blessing in disguise for the Iowa native. With events leading up to the 1919 Black Sox scandal, this probably saved his reputation.

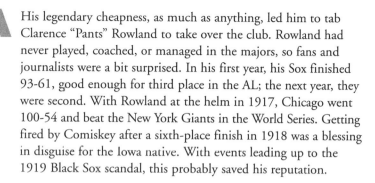

Q What would Rowland do in later years?

A He was a scout for the Cubs and served as an AL umpire. Rowland became the president of the Pacific Coast League's Los Angeles Angels and then of the league itself. West Coast baseball men were fed up with playing Santa Claus to the major leagues, losing players such as Joe DiMaggio and Ted Williams. As postwar air travel improved, it seemed inevitable that LA or San Francisco would lure a big league club. If it did not happen soon, Rowland would lead the PCL's battle cry of independence. Commissioners Kenesaw Mountain Landis and Happy Chandler fought Rowland every inch of the way, calling the PCL an outlaw league. Rowland, who lost that battle, was back in Chicago in 1954 serving as an executive with the Cubs.

Q The Sox won a weird game at Comiskey Park on July 14, 1915. What happened?

A Chicago was ahead of Philly, 4-2, in the fourth inning with rain threatening. The A's tried all they could to delay the game. Joe Bush purposely hit Red Faber with a pitch. Faber, trying to speed up the game, wanted to get thrown out by stealing, but little effort was made to retire him. He stole second, then third, and finally home. The rain never materialized, and Faber's swipe of home proved to be the game's decisive run.

Q Faber, whose 254 wins for the Sox is second only to Ted Lyons, was rather efficient against Washington on May 12, 1915. How efficient?

A He needed just 67 pitches to beat the Senators; in two of the nine innings, he retired the side with three pitches.

Q He sacrificed 44 times in 1916, which is still a team record. Who is this native of Pottstown, Pennsylvania?

A Buck Weaver, a man with jug ears and a perpetual smile on his face. He switched from shortstop to third base in 1917 and was named to *Baseball Magazine's* American League All-Star team. That season was Weaver's finest as he led the club in hitting (.284) and fielding (.949). He batted .333 in the 1917 World Series as the Sox beat the New York Giants.

Q What did the Sox do in Detroit on July 6, 1917?

A Pitchers Red Faber and Jim Scott combined to end Ty Cobb's hitting streak at 40 games in a 4-1 loss. Cobb's streak fell one game shy of tying his own AL record, established in 1912.

Q In 1917, as imperial, territorial, and economic rivalries led the United States to enter the "Great War" in which 10 million people were killed and another 20 million wounded, baseball was still being played. How did the White Sox do that year?

A Clarence Rowland's team won 100 games, finishing well ahead of second-place Boston. Attendance at Comiskey Park was 684,521, the best since 1905. The top offensive performers were Happy Felsch (.308 batting average, 6 homers, and 102 RBIs) and Eddie Collins (53 stolen bases), while Eddie Cicotte led in all the major pitching categories (28-13 record, 1.53 ERA, 346 innings pitched, and 150 strikeouts).

Q What was the Opening Day lineup for the White Sox team that would go on to win the 1917 World Series?

A Bill O'Neill (right field), Frank Isbell (second base), George Davis (shortstop), Jiggs Donahue (first base), Fielder Jones (center field), Rube Vinson (left field), George Rohe (third base), Billy Sullivan (catcher), and Frank Owen (pitcher).

Q They would face John McGraw's New York Giants that October. Did the Sox win it all for the second time in 11 years?

A They did, in six games. Cicotte started for Chicago in the opener, outdueling New York's Slim Sallee, 2-1. Ferdie Schupp, the Giants' ace, was on the mound for Game 2, but the White Sox sent him to the showers in the second inning. They went on to an easy 7-2 victory behind the pitching of Red Faber. The Series shifted to the Polo Grounds for Games 3 and 4, both of which went to the home club. Two days later in Chicago, with 27,746 fans looking on, the White Sox came back from a three-run deficit keyed by Chick Gandil's two-run double. Faber won again with two innings of perfect relief work. Farber started for a third time in Game 5, and he was up to the task, holding the Giants to six hits and two runs. The White Sox scored three times in the fourth—Gandil smacked a two-run single, and the Giants fielded poorly—and got another run in the ninth. The final score was 4-2, and they had finished off New York to capture the championship. The Giants had lost in the World Series for the fourth straight time (1911, 1912, 1913, and 1917).

Q How did "Shoeless" Joe Jackson do in the 1917 World Series?

A He batted .304, drove in two runs, and walked once. Jackson, of course, would be one of the eight players involved in the Black Sox scandal two years hence. This South Carolina native, who could barely read, played for three different major league teams during his 12-year career: the A's in 1908 and 1909, the Cleveland Indians from 1910 to mid-1915, and then through 1920 with the White Sox. Jackson, a superb left fielder, has the third-highest career batting average (.356) in history. In 1911, while in Cleveland, Jackson batted .408—the sixth-highest mark since 1901, the point at which the modern era is delineated. Babe Ruth claimed to have modeled his hitting technique after that of Jackson.

Q Who was the first Sox player to reach the Hall of Fame?

A Second baseman Eddie Collins, in 1939. He was voted in with George Sisler and Wee Willie Keeler. Collins played for Chicago from 1915 to 1925, amassing a .331 batting average. Even now, he ranks among the franchise's career leaders in several major statistical categories; Collins is second with a .426 on-base percentage, third with 1,608 singles, and fourth with 2,007 hits.

Q Who is the only player in White Sox history to hit at least 20 triples in a season?

A Joe Jackson, who did it twice. He had 21 in 1916 and 20 in 1920.

Q The 1918 Sox fell to sixth place in the American League, 17 games behind Boston. And yet some World Series games were played at Comiskey Park that year. Why?

A It served as the home field for the Chicago Cubs as they faced the Red Sox. The Cubs borrowed Comiskey Park because it was much larger than Wrigley Field. Boston, with the superbly talented but troublesome Babe Ruth, won the Series, 4-2.

The 1919 Chicago White Sox, forever remembered as the Black Sox
for throwing that year's World Series. Shoeless Joe Jackson is in the back row,
second from the right, his gloved hand draped on a teammate's shoulder.

CHAPTER TWO

SCANDAL

America experienced a boom of baseball popularity after World War I, and attendance records were being set right and left. In the case of the Chicago White Sox, the numbers are striking: Home attendance, which averaged just 3,147 in 1918, almost tripled the next year. The 1919 World Series was sure to be profitable, generating far more revenue than any other Series to date. Robust capitalism being what it was and still is, the owners would keep the lion's share of that money.

The Black Sox scandal, which started out as a few gamblers trying to get rich, became the darkest event in baseball history. It jolted a nation already in turmoil and shook the faith of baseball fans. The conspirators may be long dead, but the controversy rages on even today. First of all, it should be remembered that games had been thrown before, both by individuals and players working in concert; the first recorded instance of a fixed game was in 1877. Other World Series had been less than on the square for one reason or another. Indeed, the very first World Series, played between the Boston Red Sox and the Pittsburgh Pirates in 1903, was rumored to have been fixed.

The surprise loss of the White Sox in the 1919 Series was the subject of sub rosa talk throughout the next season as they battled the Cleveland Indians for the American League pennant. If not for a series of gutsy columns written by Hugh Fullerton, the issue might have faded away. Finally, in September 1920 a grand jury was convened in Chicago to investigate. Four players confessed but subsequently recanted. Comiskey suspended all eight implicated White Sox—Eddie Cicotte, Joe Jackson, Chick Gandil, Swede Risberg, Happy Felsch, Buck Weaver, Lefty Williams, and Fred McMullin. The move decimated the team, which finished two games behind the Indians. All eight were indicted for fraud by the grand jury but acquitted (in part because the transcripts of the confessions went missing and later turned up in the office of Comiskey's attorney) in a trial.

Major league baseball, however, would not forgive. The sport's reputation was damaged enough to cause the owners to appoint Judge

Kenesaw Mountain Landis as its first commissioner. One day after the jury's decision, Landis issued a statement that read: "Regardless of the verdict of juries, no player who throws a ball game, no player who undertakes or promises to throw a ball game, no player who sits in confidence with a bunch of crooked gamblers and does not promptly tell his club about it, will ever play professional baseball." With those thunderous words, the eight players were banned from organized baseball for life. Chicago fell to seventh place in 1921 and would finish each season through the mid-1930s in the lower half of the standings. The Sox would not be genuine contenders until the 1950s. They would win an AL pennant in 1959, but not until 2005 were they again World Series champions. Although such a long drought cannot be pinned on players who made injudicious decisions back in 1919, the shadow did linger.

Chick Gandil was born in St. Paul, Minnesota, but by age 17 he was playing ball in various towns along the Arizona–Mexico border. When did this notorious figure in franchise history first wear the pale hose?

He played 77 games for the White Sox in 1910 and was sold to Washington. While in our nation's capital, Gandil came to know Sport Sullivan, a sports gambler and bookie. Sullivan had friends even richer and more powerful than himself who would later play a part in the big scandal. Gandil spent a season with the Indians before returning to Chicago. He was the regular first baseman for three years but was also a malcontent. By all accounts a ringleader in throwing the game to the Reds, Gandil batted a paltry .233 but committed only one error in that Series.

Q "The Swede is a hard guy." Who uttered these words, and to whom did they refer?

A Shoeless Joe Jackson said them, rather fearfully, of Swede Risberg, his teammate of four years with the Sox. This rough and rangy shortstop once punched out a minor league umpire after a called third strike. Jackson sought protection after Risberg threatened to kill him if he dared talk in the 1921 trial.

Q Risberg, lieutenant to first baseman Chick Gandil in throwing the 1919 Series, was a serial offender. How so?

A He had also fixed games during his rookie year of 1917 as well as in 1920. Later in the decade, in an attempt to discredit other players (whom he dismissed as "white lilies") Risberg claimed that Detroit had thrown four games in 1917 to help Chicago clinch the flag; it was a common practice then for teams to reward others with such gifts. Another major investigation ensued, but Commissioner Landis dismissed the charges for lack of evidence. He did, however, abolish the practice of teams showing "appreciation" to others.

Q What was third baseman Buck Weaver's part in the scandal?

A Weaver was one of the best third basemen of his time, the only one against whom Ty Cobb would not bunt. He was banned not for taking part in the fix but for knowing about it and failing to tell team officials. Like the others, he was banished from the game for life. Almost until his death in 1956, he tried to clear his name but to no avail. The statistics seem to support his claim that he didn't participate in the scam: He batted .324 in the 1919 World Series with 11 hits and played errorless ball.

Q Oscar Emil "Happy" Felsch played center field for the Sox from 1915 to 1920. He, too, got caught up in the Black Sox scandal. What did he say when it was all over?

A "Well, the beans are spilled and I think I'm through with baseball. I got $5,000. I could have got just about that much by being on the level if the Sox had won the Series. And now I'm out of baseball— the only profession I know anything about, and a lot of gamblers have gotten rich. The joke seems to be on us." Over the next 15 years, Felsch would tour the country with various amateur teams. He died of liver disease in his hometown of Milwaukee in 1964 at age 72.

Q This right-handed knuckleball specialist, a Detroit native, won 208 games over the course of a 14-year career with the Tigers, Red Sox, and White Sox. Name him.

A Gap-toothed Eddie Cicotte, best known for his involvement in the Black Sox scandal. Boston sold him to Chicago on July 22, 1912. Cicotte had a breakout year in 1913, going 18-12 with an ERA of 1.58. He would lead the league in winning percentage (.682) in 1916. But his best year was 1917, when he won 28 games and led the AL in wins, ERA, and innings pitched, and tossed a no-hitter against the St. Louis Browns. That year, the White Sox beat the New York Giants in the World Series. Cicotte won Game 1, lost Game 3, and pitched six innings of relief in Game 5.

Q Abe Attell, once featherweight boxing champion, became associated with mobster Arnold Rothstein during his days in the ring. What was his link to the White Sox?

A Attell was the messenger between Rothstein and the players as the fix of the 1919 World Series was planned.

Q Who was the most conspicuously bad player for the Sox in the 1919 Series?

A Pitcher Lefty Williams, without a doubt. Joe Jackson's roommate, he was at his peak in 1919, going 23-11. Against Cincinnati, however, his skills seemingly deserted him as he lost three games, had a 6.61 ERA, and issued eight walks.

Q How did Cicotte do in that infamous year of 1919?

A Splendidly. He went 29-7 and led the Sox to the AL pennant. Cicotte's salary was $6,000, but there was a provision for a $10,000 bonus if he won 30 games. As the season came to a close, Comiskey told manager Kid Gleason to bench Cicotte, thus preventing him from winning that 30th game and the extra $10K. It was speculated that such an unkind act motivated him to participate in the fix. This, like so much else in the Black Sox scandal, is a matter of dispute.

Q Who was the least significant of the Black Sox?

A Reserve third baseman Fred McMullin, who had few chances to throw games, pinch-hitting twice in the tainted Series. One of those at-bats was for a single. McMullin became a part of the fix after overhearing several other players' conversations. He threatened to report them unless he was included. McMullin served as the Sox' advance scout for the 1919 World Series. It has been suggested that, as a way of covering himself and his fellow conspirators, McMullin compiled a flawed scouting report for all the "clean" Sox about what they might expect from the Reds. This may explain why Eddie Collins batted just .226 in the Series.

Q Two other former major leaguers were part of the fix. Who were they?

A William Thomas "Sleepy Bill" Burns and Billy Maharg. Burns was an ex-pitcher who had compiled a none-too-impressive record of 30-52 for five teams from 1908 to 1912. Maharg, who had reversed the spelling of his name (Graham) for reasons known only to him, played in one game with the Tigers in 1912 and one with the Phillies in 1916. Burns and Maharg were supposed to raise $100,000 in payoff money from Rothstein, although far less than that ever got into the hands of the players. The White Sox—who were heavily favored to win the Fall Classic—were suddenly underdogs to the Cincinnati Reds, at least in the eyes of the betting public. Thus began the cascade of dishonesty that saw the White Sox drop the 1919 World Series to the Reds in eight games.

Q How did the Series begin?

A Game 1 was played on October 1, 1919, at Redland Field in Cincinnati. A crowd of 30,511 saw Cicotte (who was paid his $10,000 the night before), on the mound in the bottom of the first inning, plunk leadoff hitter Maurice Rath in the back with just his second pitch. This was a prearranged signal to Rothstein and his confederates that the fix was on. Still, the game remained close for a while since the conspirators wished not to make their aim too obvious. In the fourth, however, Cicotte gave up several hits, including a two-out triple to the opposing pitcher, Dutch Reuther. Cincy then scored five runs to break a 1-1 tie, finally triumphing by a 9-1 score. Burns and Maharg went back to Attell for the second installment of $20,000, but they did not get it.

28

Q How did it go in Game 2?

A The players, perhaps sensing their own vulnerability, were still willing to go through with the fix—although only Cicotte had his money at this point. Lefty Williams had a shaky start but settled down and pitched well until the fourth inning, at which time he walked three Reds and gave up as many runs. After that, Williams looked unhittable, giving up just one more run. But with weak hitting—Gandil most especially—the White Sox lost, 4-2. Rothstein and Attell were still reluctant to pay up, but Burns managed to get $10,000. He passed it to Gandil, who distributed it among his fellow conspirators. The teams rode the trains to Chicago for Game 3, to be played the very next day.

Q What unsavory character had played with both the White Sox (1913 and 1914) and the Reds (1916–1918), and was one of the go-betweens in the Black Sox scandal?

A Hal Chase. He was a very talented first baseman and batter in his 15-year major league career, but Chase was widely known for his willingness to throw games for quick money.

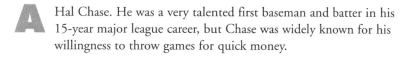

Q Things were spinning out of control by Game 3, with dissent and threats among the players. What happened at Comiskey Park?

A Dickie Kerr, the Game 3 starter, was not in on the fix. The conspirators disliked him and had originally planned to lose this game regardless of how Kerr pitched. The Sox scored early, with Gandil driving in two runs, and Kerr threw a three-hit shutout. It is not entirely clear whether they won Game 3 in spite of themselves.

Q The fourth game in four days took place on October 4, and Cicotte was back on the mound. How did he do?

A Cicotte did not want his intentions to be quite so apparent as in Game 1. He shut out Cincinnati for four innings, but in the fifth Cicotte fielded a ball and threw wildly to first base. The Reds' next batter singled to center, and Cicotte first cut off Jackson's throw home and then fumbled the ball, which allowed the run to score. Cicotte gave up a double to the next batter and the 2-0 score stood. To the amazement of most baseball fans, the Reds led the Series, 3-1. After the game, Sullivan delivered $20,000, which Gandil split equally with Jackson, Felsch, Risberg, and Williams—Chicago's Game 5 starter.

Q In Game 5, which was delayed one day due to rain, did Williams pitch like a man trying to throw a game?

A In fact, neither he nor Hod Eller of the Reds allowed a runner past first base until the sixth inning. That's when Eller hit a blooper and stretched a double into a triple thanks in part to Felsch's off-line throw. Eller soon scored, and more questionable defense from Felsch permitted two more runs. The Reds won, 4-0, and were only one game from winning the best-of-nine Series.

Q What about the White Sox' owner and manager? Did they know nothing about the skullduggery of some of their men?

A Charles Comiskey had learned of the fix, before the World Series began, from both Jackson and Kid Gleason, the team's manager. Neither of them was banned by Commissioner Landis. In fact, when Gleason learned that the rumors were true, he felt so heartbroken and betrayed that he hardly got out of bed for a week.

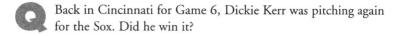

Q Back in Cincinnati for Game 6, Dickie Kerr was pitching again for the Sox. Did he win it?

A At least some of the Black Sox were ready to double-cross the double-crossers, playing to win from then on. Kerr was not as sharp as in Game 3. The Reds took advantage of three errors and had a four-run lead until Chicago tied it, 4-4, in the sixth. It went into extra innings. In the tenth, Gandil drove in Weaver with the winning run. In the simplest terms, by winning the Black Sox were forcing Sullivan, Rothstein et al. to pay up. The pressure was rising on all concerned.

Q Regardless of widespread rumors about Cicotte's first two show-ings, White Sox manager Kid Gleason trusted his ace for Game 7. Did the knuckleballer let him down?

A Not this time. Chicago scored early and, for once, the Reds committed multiple errors. They threatened briefly in the sixth but lost, 4-1, and the Series was close again. This, of course, caught the attention of Sullivan and Rothstein. The night before Game 8, Williams received a none-too-cordial visit from one of Sullivan's associates who informed him that if he did not blow the game in the first inning, bad things were sure to happen to him and his wife.

Q Did this late-night conversation have its intended effect?

A Indeed it did. In the first inning, almost every ball Williams threw was slow and right over the plate. He yielded three runs before Gleason yanked him. Relief pitcher Bill James was also ineffective—although he gave an honest effort. The Sox rallied in the eighth, but the Reds won it, 10-5, clinching the eight-game Series. Pat Moran's players celebrated in the visitors' locker room at Comiskey Park, but they too must have wondered about the legitimacy of their championship.

Q Besides Kerr and Weaver, what Chicago players did well in the '19 Series?

A Catcher Ray Schalk batted .304, was 2-for-3 with men in scoring position, scored one run and drove in two. He was also vociferous in his denunciations of Williams and Cicotte. Joe Jackson had a .375 batting average and was 5-for-12 with men in scoring position. He scored 5 runs, had 3 doubles, a home run, and 6 RBIs. Nevertheless, the degree of Jackson's involvement in the conspiracy remains unclear. Jackson, despite his confession and incriminating testimony before the grand jury, maintained his innocence and many people (such as Ted Williams) later came to his defense. Jackson handled 30 chances in the outfield but committed no errors. However, he had just one RBI in the five games the Sox lost and even that was at the end of Game 8 when the Series was virtually over. A strong defensive player, Jackson had some odd misplays during the Series. He told one sportswriter that he had given little effort during many World Series at-bats. Most damning of all, Jackson took $5,000 from the gamblers. Frantic, depressed, and drinking heavily when the Series was over, he tried to give the money back, but the damage had been done.

Q Jackson played the 1920 season carrying the burden of being part of the Black Sox scandal, but he had a most impressive year. How did he do?

A A .382 batting average, 42 doubles, 20 triples, 12 homers, and 121 RBIs.

Q What was the plaintive cry of a young boy to Jackson after the Sox' star emerged from the Cook County Courthouse in 1920?

A "Say it ain't so, Joe!"

Q Incidentally, two other players were banned by Landis in connection with this mess. Who were they?

A The aforementioned Hal Chase, who last played for the New York Giants, and Joe Gedeon of the St. Louis Browns for conspiring with the gamblers behind the Black Sox scandal.

Q Oddly enough, one of the most honest of the 1919 White Sox, Dickie Kerr, was later given a three-year ban by Landis. What was that about?

A He went 19-17 for the demoralized team in 1921. Comiskey had promised Kerr a contract of $5,000 but dropped that to $4,500, so Kerr played semi-pro ball in Texas for three years at the higher salary. Landis rescinded Kerr's ban in 1925, but he only started two games for the Sox before retiring.

Q Where did the term *Black Sox* come from?

A Strangely enough, the players had called themselves that well before the scandal happened. Comiskey was a cheapskate owner, so miserly he would not even have his team's uniforms laundered. Thus, the players' little joke.

Q Chicago once had a pitching staff with four men who won at least 20 games apiece. What year was it, and who were the players?

A The 1920 White Sox had Red Faber (23-13), Lefty Williams (22-14), Dickie Kerr (21-9), and Eddie Cicotte (21-10). More than a half-century would pass before this feat was duplicated, by the 1971 Baltimore Orioles.

Q They didn't call it the "dead-ball era" for nothing. When did the White Sox first have a player hit at least 10 home runs in a season?

A Not until 1920, when Happy Felsch had 14.

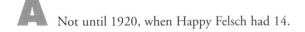

Q Identify the Philly native who had won World Series titles with the A's and Red Sox before joining Comiskey's club in 1920.

A Amos Strunk. This dependable and highly regarded center fielder had 12 pinch hits in 39 attempts in 1923, leading the American League.

Q The results of the 1919 Series were especially satisfying for one member of the Cincinnati Reds. Which one?

A Edd Roush. He had been with the White Sox briefly in 1913 but evidently failed to impress Comiskey and manager Nixey Callahan. Roush dropped down to the minors, fought his way back up, and was one of the best players in the game for more than a decade with the Reds. An acrobatic center fielder and .323 career batter, he was one player the Sox should have kept.

Q What did Jackson do after Landis made his ruling in 1921?

A He and his wife returned to Savannah, Georgia, and operated a dry cleaning business, a liquor store, and a barbecue restaurant. Jackson also played for and managed several semi-pro teams in Georgia and South Carolina. Many years after those trying times in Chicago, a poignant encounter took place in Jackson's liquor store. Former Tigers great Ty Cobb and sportswriter Grantland Rice entered to shop. Cobb made his purchase before asking, "Don't you know me, Joe?" To which Jackson replied: "Sure, I know you, Ty, but I wasn't sure you wanted to know me. A lot of them don't."

Q What were Jackson's words on his deathbed in 1951?

A "I'm about to face the greatest umpire of all, and He knows I'm innocent."

The White Sox' Ted Lyons. He never appeared in the postseason, but he helped keep the franchise afloat from 1923 to 1946, winning 260 games.

CHAPTER THREE

THE LEAN YEARS

Between 1923 and 1950, the Chicago White Sox never won a pennant. In fact, third place (three times) was the best they could manage during that span. Things might have been considerably worse if not for a couple of Southerners—pitcher Ted Lyons and shortstop Luke Appling, both of whom are enshrined in the Hall of Fame.

Born in Lake Charles, Louisiana, Lyons attended Baylor University and never played in the minor leagues. Known affectionately to Chicago baseball fans as "the Baylor Bearcat" and "Sunday Teddy," he threw a no-hitter—which took all of 67 minutes—against the Red Sox on August 21, 1926. The winner of 260 games in his big league career, he never appeared in the postseason, as his White Sox were usually in the nether regions of the American League standings. New York Yankees manager Joe McCarthy once said of him, "If Lyons had pitched for the Yankees, he would have won over 400 games."

Lyons lost velocity on his fastball in the 1930s and compensated with a nice curve. His career was extended in its later years with the help of White Sox manager Jimmy Dykes. He began using Lyons strictly on Sunday afternoons. From 1939 to 1942, the easy-going veteran started 85 games and finished 72 of them, posting a 52-30 record with a 2.96 ERA. He led the American League in ERA in his final full season of 1942 with a 2.10 mark.

After serving in the Marine Corps in World War II, Lyons was welcomed back by the Sox, even at an advanced age. He pitched a few games in early 1946 and then succeeded Dykes as the club's manager. He had less success in that role than he had as a pitcher: a meager 185-245 record in a little less than three seasons. Lyons severed his association with the Sox in 1948 and later was a pitching coach with the Tigers and Dodgers.

Appling, a native of High Point, North Carolina, nearly wound up across town with the Cubbies. He was playing with the Atlanta Crackers of the Southern Association before being sold to the Cubs late in the 1930 season. Instead, Appling joined the White Sox in a cash transaction that involved an obscure outfielder. There was nothing so special about Appling's first two seasons—especially his defensive skills: He tended to muff routine ground balls, and his arm was strong but wild.

After he took Dykes' advice and stopped trying to hit home runs in spacious Comiskey Park, Appling became a very productive and savvy leadoff man. He was renowned for fouling off pitches until he found one he liked or just drawing walks, of which he had 1,302 in his career. Appling's best year was 1936, when he led the AL with a .388 average. Never before had a White Sox player won the league's batting title, not even Joe Jackson. He did it again in 1943, at age 35.

Appling, like Lyons, suffered from a dearth of talented teammates for most of his 21-year career, never playing in the World Series. The Sox were attempting a youth movement as the 1950s began, and he was shown the door. He was a successful minor league manager, but his only job at the big league level came in late 1967 with the Kansas City Athletics, for whom he had just a 10-30 record. Appling also coached with the Indians, Tigers, Orioles, A's, White Sox, and Braves. In an old-timers' game at Washington's RFK Stadium in 1982, Appling, then 75 years old, hit a 250-foot home run off Warren Spahn.

 How did Charlie Robertson do in just his third start for the White Sox?

 Not bad. He threw the sixth perfect game in major league history on April 30, 1922, in a 2-0 defeat of the Tigers. Johnny Mostil, playing left field instead of his usual spot in center, had a diving catch to preserve the win. Play was stopped twice after Ty Cobb and Harry Heilmann registered allegations that Robertson might have been doctoring the ball. Robertson's subsequent career was fairly disappointing as he nursed a sore arm through six more seasons, losing more than he won. But he could always look back to that day in Detroit.

Q Name the first Chicago player to hit for the cycle.

A Ray Schalk did it against Detroit on June 22, 1922. The next was Jack Brohamer against Seattle on September 24, 1977.

Q After Buck Weaver was banished, the White Sox had poor play at third base for two years. That is why they were willing to pay the San Francisco Seals a record $100,000 for this man's services. Identify him.

A Willie Kamm, a player blessed with exceptional hands and good instincts. He led the American League in fielding eight times in a 13-year career and was a master of the hidden-ball trick. Kamm sometimes deflected praise of his defensive skills, crediting White Sox pitchers like Ted Lyons and Red Faber. The former's low curves and the latter's spitballs, Kamm insisted, caused hitters to send easy rollers to him at third. Kamm, who had a .281 career batting average, was known to come through in the clutch. In a poll many years later, White Sox fans named him the best third baseman in franchise history.

Q He had been the pivot man in a great infield for the Cubs, leading them to two championships. When he moved to Boston in 1914, he sparked an amazing turnaround for the "Miracle Braves," who rose from the cellar in July to winning it all in October. Name this man who managed the White Sox in the second half of the 1924 season.

A Johnny Evers.

39

Q He had been a star outfielder with the Red Sox for more than a decade and was battling with owner Harry Frazee over how he should be remunerated. Frazee dealt him for cash and two reserve outfielders to the Chicago White Sox, whose owner, Charlie Comiskey, thought that perhaps acquiring a big-name player would restore credibility to his franchise, which had been shattered by the Black Sox scandal. Who was this man with an engineering degree from the University of Vermont?

A Harry Hooper, who stayed with Chicago through the 1925 season before retiring.

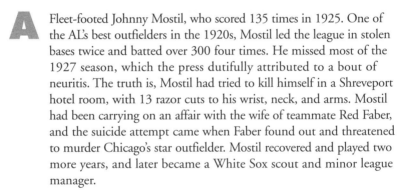

Q Who holds the Sox' record for most runs scored in a season?

A Fleet-footed Johnny Mostil, who scored 135 times in 1925. One of the AL's best outfielders in the 1920s, Mostil led the league in stolen bases twice and batted over 300 four times. He missed most of the 1927 season, which the press dutifully attributed to a bout of neuritis. The truth is, Mostil had tried to kill himself in a Shreveport hotel room, with 13 razor cuts to his wrist, neck, and arms. Mostil had been carrying on an affair with the wife of teammate Red Faber, and the suicide attempt came when Faber found out and threatened to murder Chicago's star outfielder. Mostil recovered and played two more years, and later became a White Sox scout and minor league manager.

Q This native of Ohio pitched 22 straight seasons (1914–1935) in the American League, was the Yankees' ace when they won the 1923 championship, and spent his last four years with the Sox. Who was he?

A Sam Jones, known alternately as "Sad Sam" due to his supposedly downcast expression and "Horsewhip Sam" because he threw a hard-breaking curveball.

Q What was the Chicago City Series?

A It was an exhibition game played between the White Sox and the Cubs most years between 1903 and 1942. The Sox won 20, the Cubs won 6, and there was 1 tie.

Q What pro football team called Comiskey Park home?

A The Chicago Cardinals of the NFL played home games there from 1922 to 1925 and from 1929 to 1958 before moving to St. Louis. On December 28, 1947, the Cards beat the Philadelphia Eagles there to win their first and only championship.

Q Identify the cocky and brash first baseman who broke into the majors in 1928 with three singles and a triple off Red Ruffing of the Red Sox.

A Art Shires. Captain of the team in just his second year, he twice fought manager Lena Blackburne. As the Great Depression set in, Shires sought to earn extra money by arranging boxing matches—most of which he won. But Commissioner Landis, thinking he might become involved with gamblers or underworld figures, ordered Shires to retire from the ring. After demanding a salary of $25,000 from the White Sox in 1930, Shires was promptly traded.

Q He was a reserve catcher for most of his 15-year career, peaking with the Sox in 1929 when he appeared in 106 games and batted .288. But he also spoke several languages, was widely viewed as the smartest guy in the game, and was the subject of at least three biographies. Who was he?

A Moe Berg, a Princeton grad who also earned a law degree from Columbia and studied philosophy at the Sorbonne. In the early 1930s, Berg was among a delegation of players who toured Japan, teaching the game and serving as sports ambassadors. While in Tokyo, Berg addressed the legislature—in passable Japanese. He also made a clandestine panoramic film from the tallest building in the city. It was screened by Lt. Col. Jimmy Doolittle before his 1942 raid on Tokyo. Berg took part in various cloak-and-dagger adventures during and after the war, in Central and South America, and all over Europe.

Q The White Sox and Tigers met in Chicago on May 24, 1929. How did it turn out, and what unusual thing happened?

A The Tigers prevailed, 6-5. The losing pitcher was Ted Lyons, who went all 21 innings. George Uhle went 20 for Detroit and got relief help in the 21st.

Q Was Al Capone, king of organized crime in Chicago in the 1920s, a fan of the White Sox?

A Scarface was not much of a baseball fan, but his allegiance tended toward the Cubs.

Q In 1929, the White Sox traded one of their stalwarts to the Cleveland Indians for catcher Chick Autry. Who was he, and did the trade work out?

A Augustus "Bibb" Falk had come up with the Sox briefly in 1920 and was a regular the next year, replacing the banned Joe Jackson in left field. Falk hit at least .285—with a career-high .352 in 1924—in each of his nine seasons in Chicago. The trade of Falk to Cleveland was not a good one. He batted over .300 for the Tribe for the next three seasons, while Autry did little with the Sox. After retiring, Falk coached at his alma mater, the University of Texas, winning two national championships.

Q Who was the first player in White Sox history to collect eight RBIs in a game?

A Carl Reynolds accomplished that feat in a 15-4 defeat of New York at Yankee Stadium in 1930. It would not be done by a Chicago player again for 47 years. Jim Spencer was the man, and he did it twice.

Q Identify Donie Bush and his place in White Sox history.

A Just 5' 6" and 130 pounds, he was a fine shortstop with the Tigers and Senators from 1909 to 1923. Bush was manager of the Pittsburgh Pirates when they met the fearsome 1927 Yankees in the World Series and got swept. As manager of the White Sox in 1930 and 1931, his teams finished in seventh and eighth place in the AL.

Q Lew Fonseca, who played first and second base for the Reds, Phillies, Indians, and White Sox from 1921 to 1933, had a .316 career batting average. What is his most long-lasting contribution to the game?

A As manager of the White Sox in the early 1930s, he used film extensively. Employing what then seemed like a radical idea, he analyzed baseball games and was able to find flaws in players—his own and those of opposing managers. But in three seasons as the Sox' skipper, he never won more than 67 games.

Q Who owned the club after the Old Roman died in 1931?

A His son, J. Louis Comiskey, inherited the White Sox. He owned the team until his death in 1939. The First National Bank, executor of his will, revealed that the club had lost $675,000 over the past 11 years and sought to force a sale. Instead, it passed on to his widow, Grace Comiskey. She owned the team for 17 years until her death in 1956, at which time her daughter, Dorothy Comiskey, succeeded her as the club's principal owner; she owned 54 percent, while the remainder was in the hands of her brother, Charles, Jr. They would battle in court over control of the franchise. Dorothy, the wife of former pitcher John Rigney, sold her stake in the club to Bill Veeck in 1959 for $2.7 million. He owned it for three years before illness forced him to sell to Arthur Allyn in 1961 for $3.25 million. Allyn, a LaSalle Street stockbroker, had made the deal for its tax breaks as much as anything. He was the owner for eight years, at which time his brother, John, bought it to prevent the franchise shifting to Milwaukee. During John Allyn's tenure, cash woes almost forced him to miss payroll a few times. He sold controlling interest back to Veeck in 1975 (for $10 million) but kept a 20 percent interest. Jerry Reinsdorf, a real estate investor, and Eddie Einhorn, a television executive, bought it from Veeck six years later for $20 million and are the current owners.

Q The White Sox and the New York Giants played an exhibition game at Buffs Stadium in Houston on February 21, 1931. What was unique about it?

A This game, the score of which has been lost to the mists of time, was the first the Sox played under the lights. Eight years would pass before the Sox had a night game at Comiskey Park.

Q On May 30, 1932, the Indians beat the White Sox in a double-header, 12-6 and 12-11. What made that day in Cleveland so memorable?

A When the second game was over, various members of the Chicago team claimed that umpire George Moriarty's calls had favored the Tribe. Moriarty defended his honor under the stands, knocking down pitcher Milt Gaston, but getting whipsawed by manager Lew Fonseca and catchers Charlie Berry and Frank Grube. He had to be taken to a local hospital.

Q The Philadelphia A's were struggling to stay afloat during the Great Depression, so they sold three of their best players for $100,000 to the Sox after the 1932 season. Who were they?

A Third baseman Jimmy Dykes, and outfielders Mule Haas and Al Simmons.

Q What was Dykes' baseball background?

A He spent 44 years in the majors as a player, manager, and coach. Playing for his hometown A's, he had won a pair of World Series (1929 and 1930). With the Sox, Dykes became player/manager early in the 1934 season. His contributions as a player dwindled —his final game was in 1939—but Dykes must have pleased owner Charles Comiskey, Jr., because he was the team's skipper through 1946. Dykes still holds the franchise record for most games managed, most wins, and most losses. But his winning percentage, .489, is nowhere near the top. As a manager, he was combative and argu-mentative, often getting fined and suspended. Dykes went on to manage the A's, Orioles, Reds, Tigers, and Indians. He never won a pennant, and his highest finish was third place.

Q What unique personnel move did Dykes make in 1945?

A Dykes was a master umpire-baiter and bench-jockey, as were two of his long-time teammates and coaches, Mule Haas and Bing Miller. Dykes considered this now-lost art to be a key component of the game. So he hired Karl Scheel to assist him and his coaches in verbally abusing the umps and opposing players. Scheel was a Marine veteran of World War II who had a booming voice. Ostensibly put on the staff to pitch batting practice, Scheel did his job well, earning two ejections and instigating a brawl in a game with the St. Louis Browns.

Q He was a devastating hitter over a nine-year stretch with the Philadelphia A's, topping .380 four times, and was equally effective in the field. He had a warm spot in Connie Mack's heart, but that did not prevent a trade to the ChiSox in 1933. Who was this man of proud Polish ancestry?

A Al Simmons, born Aloys Szymanski. He called Comiskey Park home for three years. Then he was off to play for Detroit, Washington, the Boston Braves, Cincinnati, the Philadelphia A's, and the Boston Red Sox.

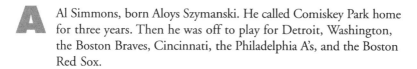

Q Name the former MVPs (of either league) who later joined the White Sox.

A Eddie Collins (1914 with the Philadelphia A's), Johnny Evers (1914/Cubs), Roger Peckinpaugh (1925/Senators), Phil Cavaretta (1945/Cubs), Bob Elliot (1947/Braves), Ken Boyer (1964/Cardinals), George Foster (1977/Reds), George Bell (1987/Blue Jays), and Jose Canseco (1988/A's).

Q What happened in team history on January 19, 1934?

A Shoeless Joe Jackson's appeal for reinstatement was turned down by Commissioner Landis.

Q The White Sox made a smart move in 1935 when they bought a catcher from the St. Louis Browns. He gave them three good years behind the plate, hitting .285 in 1936 and leading AL catchers with 87 assists the next season. Who was this graduate of the University of Alabama?

A Luke Sewell. In a career that lasted two decades, he never struck out more than 27 times.

Q In 1935, his first full year in the majors, he pitched a no-hitter for the Sox against the Indians. Name this individual.

A Vern Kennedy. He would follow with a 21-9 record in 1936, despite a league-high 147 walks. Kennedy soon developed a sore arm, got traded to Detroit in 1939, and lost 20 games. He was able to extend his career with five more teams through the mid-1940s. Kennedy, a native of Kansas City, was honored when his alma mater, the University of Central Missouri, named its football field after him.

Q Where could Ted Lyons be found in late October 1935?

A He was in Mexico City, where a touring group of American League all-stars (including Rogers Hornsby, Jimmie Foxx, and Vern Kennedy) met the Negro League champions, the Pittsburgh Crawfords (with greats like Oscar Charleston, Josh Gibson, Judy Johnson, and Cool Papa Bell). The AL squad won two and tied one.

Q Who led the Sox in home runs every year from 1934 to 1937?

A Zeke Bonura, a native of New Orleans who was a fine slugger but a nonchalant fielder. In fact, Bonura led AL first basemen in fielding in 1936 by refusing to go after any ball that did not come directly to him. A colorful and outspoken man, Bonura aggravated team officials with his annual holdouts. He was traded to the Senators in 1938 for these reasons and because of rumors that he fancied the daughter of owner J. Louis Comiskey.

Q How significant was it when Appling won the 1936 AL batting crown?

A It was remarkable on at least three levels: (1) Never before had a shortstop won that honor. (2) He was the first White Sox player to do so. (3) His .388 average in the '36 season remains the highest batting average for a shortstop in baseball history.

Q What pitcher halted Luke Appling's 27-game hitting streak in 1936?

A Wes Ferrell of the Red Sox did it on September 3 of that year. Appling's streak remained a franchise record until Albert Belle broke it in 1997.

Q Monty Stratton, a 6' 5" Texan, won 30 games for Chicago in 1937 and 1938. What tragedy then befell him?

A Shortly after the 1938 season, Stratton, nicknamed "Gander," was hunting rabbits on the family farm when he fell and accidentally discharged a holstered pistol. This resulted in enough damage to his right leg to require amputation. Stratton, now wearing a prosthesis, worked with the White Sox the next two seasons as a coach and batting practice pitcher. With the onset of World War II, he tried to enlist but was rejected. He soon organized a semi-pro team in Greenville, Texas, and worked assiduously to improve his coordination on the field. In 1946, eight years after the accident, Stratton was pitching again. Although other teams persistently bunted balls out of his reach, Stratton was able to win 18 games one year in the lower minors. His courage and fortitude were the subject of a 1949 film in which Jimmy Stewart played him.

Q This right-handed pitcher was with the Sox from 1937 to 1947, minus the war years. He was on the mound on August 14, 1939, for the first night game ever at Comiskey Park. Identify him.

A Johnny Rigney. In 1941, just before leaving for military duty he married the daughter of the White Sox' president. Rigney returned to the team older and with a sore arm, so he moved into the White Sox' front office, eventually becoming vice president.

Q Name the right-handed junk-baller, a member of the White Sox from 1936 to 1940, who threw underhand, sidearm, and three-quarters.

A Clint Brown, whose 61 appearances (56 of which he finished) in 1939 set a major league record for relievers.

Q How did it go for the White Sox in the 1940 season opener?

A It was a cold day at Comiskey Park as the Indians' 21-year-old Bob Feller threw a no-hitter.

Q This broad-shouldered outfielder, a North Carolina native, showed considerable hitting promise for the Senators in his first two years but was sent to the Sox prior to the 1940 season—perhaps because his defensive skills were barely adequate. Name him.

A Taffy Wright, who compiled a .311 career batting average. He was with Chicago six years, split in half by military service in World War II.

Q It was supposedly the longest home run in the history of Comiskey Park. Who was responsible for this prodigious clout?

A On May 14, 1940, the Red Sox and White Sox were tied at 6 in the 10th inning. Johnny Rigney delivered, and Boston's Jimmie Foxx turned it around. The ball went over the left field roof as the first-place BoSox celebrated.

Q What first baseman tied a club record by hitting 27 home runs in 1940?

A Joe Kuhel, who twice scored more than 100 runs in his six years in Chicago.

Q This man came from Hazelton, Pennsylvania, served as the White Sox' primary catcher from 1939 to 1948, and was the father of a future New York Yankee. Who was he?

A Mike Tresh, who homered just twice in a career lasting 1,027 games. His son was Tom Tresh, an outfielder with the Bronx Bombers in the 1960s.

Q Lyons was adored by the fans in Chicago. Give us an example.

A The *Chicago Tribune* sponsored a "Ted Lyons Day" in 1940. The newspaper asked fans to send a dime each toward a gift for the easy-going pitcher, and the response was overwhelming as the *Tribune* had enough dimes (surely some gave quarters and 50-cent pieces) to buy Lyons a Buick convertible.

Q Rookie shortstop Chico Carrasquel had a 24-game hitting streak in 1950. How did it come to an end?

A On August 6 of that year, Ellis Kinder was on the mound for the Red Sox, and he halted Carrasquel's streak in a 9-2 victory.

Q On June 28, 1941, this rookie had one of the finest single-game performances in club history in a 6-4 defeat of the Indians. He swiped four bases—including second, third, and home in the ninth inning—and hit a pair of home runs. Identify him.

A Second baseman Don Kolloway, who entered that game against Cleveland with a .168 batting average.

Q What frightening episode did Charles Comiskey, Jr.'s, wife experience on February 23, 1942?

A She went to Ted Lyons' bowling alley in Chicago. While in the waiting room, the matriarch was taken at gunpoint by two men. The perps divested her of a $3,500 diamond ring and drove her around for 45 minutes. They let her keep $1 for cab fare and released her unharmed.

Q This lanky right-handed pitcher was with the White Sox the entire decade of the 1940s. No fewer than 43 of his 63 victories came between 1943 and 1945, when major league baseball was anything but dynamic. Name him.

A Orval Grove, a native of Mineral, Kansas.

Q What player with the 1943 White Sox led the league in stolen bases (56) and triples (12)?

A Wally Moses.

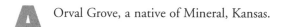

Q Who was known as "Steady Eddie" and the "Junk Man"?

A Ed Lopat, a member of the White Sox from 1944 to 1948 before a trade to the Bronx, where he helped the Yanks procure five World Series titles. Lacking any pretense of a fastball, he frustrated hitters and kept them off balance with a bewildering assortment of slow breaking pitches with cunning effect. Free-swinging teams like Cleveland were easy victims; Lopat had a 40-12 lifetime mark against the Indians. He later served as manager of the Kansas City A's.

Q The career of this Long Island native was winding down before he joined the Sox during the war years. Despite batting .308 in 1945, he was cut. Name him.

A Tony Cuccinello, who, upon getting his release, described himself as "the most surprised guy in baseball." He would return to the team in 1957 as a coach under his former teammate, Al Lopez.

Q A fairly historic event took place at Comiskey Park on July 5, 1947. What was it?

A Larry Doby of the Cleveland Indians became the American League's first black player (if we choose not to include the aforementioned Bobby Estellela and other Caribbean stars with the Senators in the 1930s), four months after Jackie Robinson had done the same with the Brooklyn Dodgers of the NL. He came to bat once, as a pinch hitter, and struck out as the White Sox won, 6-5. The next day, Doby went 1-for-5 in his first full game at first base.

Q Ike Pearson was with the Phillies for five years before finishing up with one season, 1948, in Chicago. What dubious record did Pearson set in his career?

A He ended with a record of 13-50; his .206 winning percentage remains the worst in major league history for a pitcher with at least 50 losses.

Q What ChiSox Hall of Famer hailed from tiny St. Thomas Township, Pennsylvania?

A Jacob Nelson "Nellie" Fox. This slick-fielding second baseman was 20 when he first joined the Philadelphia Athletics, and in three seasons he never became a full-time starter. Connie Mack traded him to the White Sox in 1949, and his career took off. Over the next 14 seasons, he would make the All-Star team 12 times and be chosen American League MVP in 1959. In the World Series, Fox batted a team-high .375 with three doubles, but the Sox lost to the Dodgers in six games. Fox, who won three Gold Gloves, was well complemented those years by the presence of a pair of fine shortstops, Chico Carrasquel and then Luis Aparicio. For many a season, the Sox had the best defensive infield in the league.

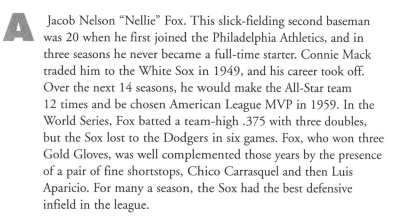

Q What was the Bard's Room?

A That was the press lounge/dining room/bar in the catacombs of Comiskey Park. Full of photos and mementoes, the Bard's Room was redolent of White Sox history.

Q Frank C. Lane became the White Sox' GM in 1948 and would hold that job for the next seven years. What was his baseball background?

A He was born in Cincinnati, played pro football for several Ohio teams before the NFL was created, and then worked as a referee in both football and basketball. Lane became the Cincinnati Reds' traveling secretary in 1933, and was the GM for the minor league Durham Bulls and Kansas City Blues before serving in World War II. He was president of the American Association for two years, at which time Comiskey hired Lane and asked him to turn a mediocre franchise into a contender.

Q How did Chicago sportswriter Dave Condon feel about Lane's hiring?

A He wrote that it was "the birth of a wonderful White Sox era. Almost from the day he set foot in the fading Baseball Palace of the World, Frantic Frankie kept the pot boiling. A man dedicated to clearing away the old wood, the old ideas, the old plumbing, and bringing in fresh faces." Lane's hiring did in fact precipitate a vast number of trades (241, to be precise) and other changes on the South Side. Within a few years, his management resulted in what would be known throughout the big leagues as the "Go-Go Sox."

Q Three pitchers won at least 10 games for the 1949 White Sox. Who were they?

A Bill Wight (15-13), Randy Gumpert (13-16), and Bob Kuzava (10-6). The top reliever that year was Max Surkont (3-5).

Q It's safe to say that Pete Seerey is not a major name in Chicago White Sox lore. And yet he did something quite major, which none others in team history have done. What was his great feat?

A On July 18, 1948, Seerey became the fifth major league player to hit four home runs in a game. The 5' 10", 200-pound Oklahoma native blasted two mammoth shots off Philadelphia's Carl Scheib, and one each off Bob Savage and Lou Brissie in the 11-inning, 12-11 Sox victory. With 16 total bases, he tied an AL record. Seerey's free-swinging ways drove his managers crazy. Consider that in 1,815 career at-bats, he struck out almost 500 times— a truly horrendous percentage.

Q Born and raised in the Windy City, he was working as a popcorn vendor at Comiskey Park for the Joe Louis–Jim Braddock heavyweight championship boxing match in 1937 the night before he signed with the Sox. He was the starting third baseman in 1940 but missed three seasons for military service before returning to play in the outfield. Name him.

A Bob Kennedy. Traded to the Indians early in the 1948 season, he batted .301 the rest of the way and helped them win the World Series. When his 16-year playing career was over, Kennedy managed the Cubs and the A's, and served as the GM of the Cubs and Astros. His son, Terry, was a fine catcher for St. Louis, San Diego, Baltimore, and San Francisco from 1978 to 1991.

Q The 1950 All-Star Game was played at Comiskey Park. How did it conclude?

A With a 14th-inning home run by Red Schoendienst of St. Louis; the NL won it by a 4-3 margin.

57

Q What diminutive southpaw was acquired by the White Sox from the Tigers prior to the 1949 season in a lopsided deal for journeyman catcher Aaron Robinson?

A Billy Pierce, and to make matters worse, the Tigers threw in $10,000. Pierce would wear the White Sox uniform for 13 years and was a pitching anchor, throwing four one-hitters. In 1953, he had seven shutouts and pitched 51 straight innings without giving up an earned run. He recorded 186 strikeouts that year, which was tops in the AL.

Q Chicago infielder Floyd Baker had a 13-year career and took part in 874 games. How many home runs did Baker hit during that time?

A One—on May 4, 1949, in an 8-7 loss to the Senators. He hit it off Sid Hudson into "Home Run Lane," named for GM Frank Lane. The mighty blast fell short of the stands but went over the wire fence, which Lane had brought in 20 feet from the stands in a feeble effort to help his team's offense.

Q Name the blond, brawny Texan who hit 29 homers in 1950 to break Zeke Bonura's franchise record.

A Gus Zernial. The very next year, he was sent to the Athletics in a three-way deal that brought Minnie Minoso to Chicago. In the 1950s, the only American Leaguers to hit more home runs than Zernial were Mickey Mantle, Yogi Berra, and Larry Doby.

Q Who was known as "Old Aches and Pains"?

A Appling, who frequently moaned about sore ankles, the flu, pink eye, and a chronic bad back. We know that during his 21-year career, he suffered a broken finger and a broken leg. Hypochondriac or not, Appling usually led the Sox in games played and managed to bat .301 at age 42. For a long time, he held the AL record for most games played at shortstop.

Q When was pioneering sportscaster Bob Elson's first game with the White Sox?

A In 1929, but he did double duty with the Sox and Cubs. Elson served in the Navy during World War II, but his popularity was such that President Franklin D. Roosevelt asked him to come home to announce the 1943 World Series. Elson worked exclusively with the Sox until 1970.

Q He was a power hitter but lead-footed in the extreme, earning 1950 rookie of the year honors with the Red Sox. He also played with the Tigers, the White Sox (1955–1958), the Reds, and the Orioles. Name him if you can.

A Walt Dropo. He is best known for a brilliant stretch in July 1952 while he was with Detroit. Dropo collected 12 consecutive hits to tie a major league record. That included a doubleheader against Washington in which he went 7-for-7.

Second baseman Nellie Fox and shortstop Luis Aparicio
execute a double play for the White Sox.

CHAPTER FOUR

GO-GO SOX

Paul Richards, who had been a reserve catcher with the Dodgers, Giants, A's, and Tigers, learned a few things along the way. Given his first chance to manage in the big leagues in 1951, he showed himself to be a brilliant and innovative strategist, an astute judge of talent, and a skilled teacher. That year, his White Sox went 81-73, a 21-game improvement over the 1950 club. Attendance at Comiskey Park jumped from 781,330 to 1,328,234. Richards was the man in the dugout when the term *Go-Go Sox* was first introduced. It referred to the team's willingness to counter power—meaning the New York Yankees—with defense, speed, and pitching.

If the White Sox were still bridesmaids, they were at least competitive again. It would be 1968 before they would drop below .500. These Chicago teams were characterized by men like left fielder Minnie Minoso, second baseman Nellie Fox, shortstop Luis Aparicio, catcher Sherman Lollar, and pitchers Billy Pierce and Virgil Trucks. The Sox were never more go-go than in 1959, when they won their first pennant in 40 years. By this time, the roster had been augmented by pitcher Early Wynn (winner of that year's Cy Young Award) and slugging first baseman Ted Kluszewski. Al Lopez, whose Cleveland Indians had won the AL pennant five years earlier, used all his moxie to get the Sox over the hump—although the Dodgers did not cooperate in the World Series.

Bill Veeck's ongoing health problems precipitated a sale of the team to the Allyn brothers in 1961. Although they could never match the entertainment skills of "Barnum Bill," their Sox continued to prosper. In 1964, the team won 98 games, including their last nine straight, but finished a game behind the pennant-winning Yanks. Eddie Stanky's 1967 club came close too, leading the AL for most of the season before being overtaken by the Red Sox, Twins, and Tigers.

And just like that, the Go-Go era was over. The team finished 36, 29, and 42 games in back of the AL winner over the next three years. Attendance dropped precipitously, and it appeared that the White Sox franchise had one foot in the grave.

Q In a 20-year career (1928–1947) with the Robins/Dodgers, Bees/Braves, Pirates, and Indians, he set a record for most games behind the plate. Other than that, his numbers were modest. He made bigger contributions as a manager, with Cleveland and Chicago. Name this son of Spanish-Cuban-American immigrants.

A Al Lopez, also known as "El Señor." His Indians won 111 games en route to the 1954 AL flag, and he was in the dugout when the Go-Go Sox won it five years later. As such, he was the only manager to interrupt the Yankees' string of AL pennants between 1949 and 1964. With a .584 career winning percentage, he ranks fourth in major league history among managers with at least 2,000 games. Lopez, over the course of 15 full seasons as manager, never had a losing record.

Q What further involvement did Lopez have with the White Sox?

A After the 1965 season, he took an advisory post with the team. But his successor, Eddie Stanky, quit in July 1968, so Lopez was back in the dugout. He stayed through the first 17 games of the 1969 season, finally retiring because of a stomach illness. Lopez was 97 and living in Tampa when he found himself back in the spotlight in 2005. Sportswriters were seeking the memories and observations of the man who had guided the Sox to the 1959 AL pennant. He died a few days after Chicago beat Houston in the World Series.

Q Identify the first black player in White Sox history.

A Saturnino Orestes Armas Miñoso Arrieta, best known in the United States as Minnie Minoso. He was born on November 29, 1922, in Havana and had played in Mexico (where he was called "el Charro Negro"—"the Black Cowboy") and in the Negro Leagues before signing with the already-integrated Cleveland Indians in 1948. Minoso was traded to the White Sox early in the 1951 season and soon became the team's regular left fielder.

Q How did he do in Chicago?

A Minoso played virtually every game for seven seasons. His batting average never dropped below .281, he excelled on the basepaths, he was a superior defensive player, and the fans loved him. He went on to play for the Cardinals and Senators, and returned to play with the Indians and White Sox. Minoso made token appearances with Chicago in 1976 (eight at-bats) and 1980 (two) in a somewhat bogus way of saying he had played pro ball in five and then six decades.

Q How did the team honor him on September 30, 1990?

A Prior to the final game at old Comiskey Park, Minoso presented the White Sox' lineup card to the umpires at home plate. He did so while wearing the uniform debuted by the White Sox, which had his familiar number 9. He, like Charles Comiskey, Nellie Fox, Luis Aparicio, and Carlton Fisk, has a life-sized statue in the center-field plaza at U.S. Cellular Field.

Q What two Chicago players posed with Marilyn Monroe in a 1951 photo, ostensibly giving her baseball tips?

A Pat Dobson and Gus Zernial. MM was holding a baseball bat while wearing a beret on her head, with short-shorts and high heels.

Q What happened in franchise history on July 29, 1951?

A More than 70,000 fans at Yankee Stadium saw New York sweep the White Sox, 8-3 and 2-0. In the opener, Joe DiMaggio hit a pair of homers off Lew Kretlow, and former Chicago hurler Bob Kuzava outpitched Saul Rogovin to win the nitecap.

Q On the last day of July 1951, the Sox dropped a 4-2 decision to the A's—their 10th loss in 11 games. But they got a good showing from their journeyman third baseman. Who was he?

A Hank Majeski, who had three hits and scored three runs. Three years later, playing for the Cleveland Indians against the New York Giants in the World Series, Majeski would stroke a pinch-hit home run.

Q This Wisconsin native served 20 seasons—a franchise record—from the 1940s to the 1960s, and was the driving force behind the great pitching staffs of the Go-Go Sox era. He had a hand in developing the White Sox farm system as well as resurrecting the careers of many vets. Who was he?

A Ray Berres.

Q He was not the first Venezuelan to reach the major leagues (his uncle, Alex Carrasquel [Washington in 1939] and Chucho Ramos [Cincinnati in 1944] preceded him), but he was certainly a great one. Name this fine shortstop out of Caracas.

A Alfonso "Chico" Carrasquel. He had been signed by the Brooklyn Dodgers in 1949, but his inability to speak English led Branch Rickey to ship him to the White Sox. GM Frank Lane took care of that problem by signing a bilingual Cuban relief pitcher named Luis Aloma to serve as translator between Carrasquel and manager Paul Richards and his teammates. Carrasquel had the unenviable task of replacing Luke Appling at shortstop, but he quickly established his bonafides. He and Nellie Fox made an excellent double-play combination.

Q What was Carrasquel's best year in Chicago?

A He had several, but his best statistically was 1954 when he posted career highs in home runs (12), RBIs (62), hits (158), runs (106), and walks (85). Prior to the 1956 season, he was dealt to the Indians to make room for another Venezuelan shortstop, Luis Aparicio. Carrasquel, who later played with the A's and Orioles, is a legend back home in Venezuela, a very influential figure for many country-men such as Aparicio, Dave Concepcion, Cesar Tovar, Ozzie Guillen, Vic Davalillo, Tony Armas, Magglio Ordonez, Bobby Abreu, Manny Trillo, Bo Diaz, Andres Galarraga, and Omar Vizquel.

Q What Chicago outfielder had a 22-game hitting streak in 1953?

A Sam Mele, who would later lead the Minnesota Twins to the 1965 AL pennant.

Q Virgil Trucks won 32 games for the Sox in 1954 and 1955, but he is best remembered for something he did while with Detroit. What was it?

A In 1952, he pitched two no-hitters for the Tigers.

Q How did "Jungle Jim" Rivera come by his nickname?

A It was given to him by a sportswriter at the *Chicago Sun-Times,* for Rivera's exuberant playing style: sliding into bases headfirst, running the bases with abandon, and making game-saving catches in right field. The son of Puerto Rican immigrants, Rivera was with the Sox from 1952 to 1961 and led the American League in stolen bases in 1955.

Q He joined the White Sox in an eight-player deal with the Browns in 1952 and was the team's primary catcher for the next decade. Who was this native of Durham, Arkansas?

A Sherman Lollar, who excelled on defense, could handle pitchers with aplomb, and was a dangerous hitter despite being painfully slow. His best season with the bat came in 1959, when he hit 22 homers and had 84 RBIs.

Q Recount the brilliant pitchers' duel between the White Sox and Tigers on August 13, 1954.

A It was scoreless for 16 innings as Chicago's Jack Harshman and Detroit's Al Aber went head to head. The Sox won it when Minnie Minoso hit a triple, driving in Nellie Fox. Harshman struck out 12 and ran his streak of consecutive scoreless innings pitched to 28.

Q How did Cass Michaels' 12-year career come to an end?

A On August 27, 1954, the Sox' third baseman was up to bat against Marion Fricano of the A's. Michaels was hit by one of Fricano's pitches, suffered a fractured skull, and never played major league baseball again.

Q Who was Chicago's top batsman in 1954?

A Minnie Minoso (.320), who hit 19 home runs and drove in 116 runs. He led the team in all three categories.

Q What Cuban-born reliever went 16-3 in 1954, leading the major leagues in won-lost percentage?

A Sandy Consuegra.

Q What did Sherman Lollar do in a game against Kansas City on April 23, 1955?

A He became the third player in major league history to collect two hits in one inning twice in the same game. Lollar slugged a pair of homers and had five RBIs as the Sox defeated the A's, 29-6. This was the first time the White Sox played a series in Kansas City (the Athletics had just moved from Philadelphia). Perhaps more significant, it was the first time the Sox flew to a major league game.

Q This late bloomer did not win a game in four short trials with the Braves and Tigers. Traded to Chicago in 1955, he mastered the slider and won 58 times over the next four years. Who was he?

A Dick Donovan, who later pitched for the Senators and Indians.

Q The White Sox had the AL rookie of the year in 1956. Who was he?

A Luis Aparicio, a Venezuelan-born shortstop. He was heavily scouted by the Cleveland Indians, but Chicago GM Frank Lane, at the suggestion of Chico Carrasquel, got involved. Lane offered Aparicio a $5,000 bonus and $5,000 in salary. He proved himself in the minors and then took over from Carrasquel at short. He also led the AL stolen bases in his debut year. In fact, Aparicio would do so every season from 1956 through 1964.

Q Is it safe to say that Aparicio was a good defensive player?

A Truer words were never spoken. Aparicio set a new standard for shortstops, winning nine Gold Gloves, and displaying verve and savvy for the Go-Go Sox. After being dealt to Baltimore, he aided the Orioles' drive to a title in 1966, returned to Chicago, and then finished up with the Red Sox. Aparicio's most productive year at the plate came in 1970 (during his second stint in Chicago), when he batted .312 and scored 86 runs. Upon his retirement in 1973, Aparicio held a number of important marks: most assists, double plays, and games played by a shortstop. When he went into the Hall of Fame 11 years later, he was the first native of South America to be so honored.

Q In the late 1950s, the center field scoreboard at Comiskey Park featured a prominent ad for tobacco products. What did it say?

A "Chesterfield! It's a hit!"

Q For whom did the Sox trade Chico Carrasquel in October 1955?

A He and pitcher Jim Busby were sent to Cleveland in return for Larry Doby.

Q Almost certainly the White Sox' most colorful owner, he ran the team from 1959 to 1961 and a second time, from 1976 to 1980. To whom do we refer?

A Bill Veeck, which, as he always liked to say, rhymes with "wreck." Best known for his flamboyant publicity stunts, which included giving away live pigs, beer, and cases of food, scoreboards with exploding fireworks, and weddings at home plate, Veeck was actually a sound baseball man. His father had been president of the Cubs, and that's where he worked as a vendor, ticket seller, and junior groundskeeper. It was Veeck who planted the ivy on the outfield walls of Wrigley Field. Previously the owner of the Indians and the Browns, in 1959 Veeck organized a syndicate that paid $2.7 million to Dorothy Comiskey Rigney, granddaughter of the Old Roman, for her controlling share of the franchise. Her brother, Charles, failed in his attempt to match the bid, and Comiskey family control ended after 60 years.

Q When most pitchers come to bat, the defenders can relax. Was Wynn an automatic out?

A He was not. A dangerous switch hitter, Wynn batted .270 or better five times, hit 17 home runs (including one grand slam), and drove in 173 runs. His managers sent him up to pinch hit 90 times. Early Wynn was one of the best-hitting pitchers the game has ever seen.

Q Where did Pierce conclude his career?

A He was traded to the San Francisco Giants in 1961 and helped them win the '62 NL pennant. Pierce had a three-hit victory over the Yankees in Game 6 of that Series.

Q Who once said that in a tight situation, with the game in the balance, he'd deck his own mother if she were up at bat?

A Early Wynn, who had a long career (1939–1963) with the Senators, Indians, and White Sox. Armed with a blazing fastball, a curveball, a slider, a changeup, a knuckleball, and a hard-nosed attitude, he was among the fiercest pitchers in the game. According to legend, he also claimed he'd throw at his grandmother because "grandma could really hit."

Q What did Wynn do in 1957 and 1958 that had never been done before?

A He became the first major league pitcher to lead his league in strikeouts in consecutive years with different teams (184 with the Indians, 189 with the White Sox). Wynn would also win the Cy Young Award in 1959 at the age of 39, posting a record of 22-10 and a 3.16 ERA as the Sox won the pennant.

Q Billy Pierce, a seven-time All-Star, missed his chance at baseball immortality against the Senators in the summer of 1958. What happened?

A He had a perfect game through 8⅔ innings. That's when Washington's backup catcher, Ed Fitz Gerald, was sent in to pinch-hit. He proceeded to whack a Pierce curveball down the right field line for a double. Pierce, undeterred, then fanned Albie Pearson for a 3-0, one-hit, victory.

Q What did the Sox do in the seventh inning of a game against the Athletics on April 22, 1959?

A They scored 11 runs on just one hit. The frame featured 3 errors, 10 walks, 1 hit batsman, a stolen base, and a single by Johnny Callison. KC had led, 6-1, after two innings but lost the game by a score of 20-6.

Q What was one of Bill Veeck's goofiest stunts?

A The date was May 26, 1959, and the place was Comiskey Park. Shortly before the White Sox and Indians began play, a helicopter landed behind second base. Four midgets dressed as spacemen jumped out. They purported to "capture" Nellie Fox and Luis Aparicio. Amusing, but it didn't help the cause as the Tribe won, 3-0. One of the tiny men was 3' 7" Eddie Gaedel, who had been sent up to pinch-hit in a game eight years earlier when Veeck owned the St. Louis Browns.

Q What happened in Sox history on September 22, 1959?

A Luis Aparicio fielded a ground ball off the bat of Cleveland's Vic Power and threw to first to clinch the White Sox' first pennant in 40 years. Early Wynn got the "W," and Al Smith homered for the new AL champs.

Q After the White Sox won the 1959 pennant, what did Chicago Mayor Richard J. Daley do?

A Daley, a lifelong fan of the Sox, told his fire chief to set off the city's air raid sirens. Many people were fearful and confused since this was the peak of the Cold War. Soon, however, they relaxed and joined in the celebration.

Q What happened to left fielder Al Smith in the fifth inning of Game 2 of the 1959 World Series?

A As he stood at the wall at Comiskey Park, watching Charlie Neal's home run leave the yard, Smith was drenched with beer spilled by a distracted Sox fan.

Q What was Jim Rivera's big defensive play in the 1959 World Series?

A In Game 5, he snagged Charlie Neal's long drive to preserve a 1-0 Sox victory before some 90,000 screaming Dodgers fans. No doubt, Jungle Jim was a character. Once, after Chicago had beaten the Kansas City A's, he had this to say to former first lady Bess Truman: "I'm sure sorry my homer beat your team, but it was a hell of a wallop, eh, Bess?"

Q Norm Cash was a second-year man with the 1959 AL champion White Sox, but he didn't play much. He was sent to Cleveland and from there to Detroit. How did he do with the Tigers?

A Cash spent 15 years in Motown, hit 373 home runs, and was consistently one of the best first basemen in the majors. The Sox should have kept him.

Q Bob Shaw, whose 18-6 record was the AL's best in 1959, was a fine pitcher but also a thorn in the side of management wherever he went. What did he do when Bill Veeck refused to give him the raise he felt he deserved?

A He stood atop a catwalk inside Comiskey Park and shouted to fans, "We're not going to win! Why are you people here?" Shaw was soon on his way out of Chi-town.

Q This muscle-bound first baseman was from the Chicago area, played football at the University of Indiana, and had several good years with the Cincinnati Reds before injuries started to take a toll. He spent a season and a half in Pittsburgh before the Sox acquired him for some added punch in the drive to the 1959 AL pennant. Name him.

A Ted Kluszewski. In the first game of the World Series at Comiskey Park, "Klu" blasted two home runs and had 5 RBIs in an 11-0 rout of the Dodgers. LA won the next four games with strong pitching that neutralized Chicago's hitters—except for Kluszewski, who batted .391.

Who was Walter E. Jagiello?

This polka musician from the South Side of Chicago penned the 1959 anthem, "Let's Go-Go-Go White Sox." The first stanza is as follows: "White Sox! White Sox! / Go-Go White Sox! / Let's Go-Go-Go White Sox / We're with you all the way! / You're always in there fighting / And you do your best / We're glad to have you / Out here in the Middle West."

What was new with the Sox's uniforms on Opening Day 1960?

Owner Bill Veeck unveiled new road uniforms with the players' names above the number on the back. A popular innovation, this was soon applied to home unis, too. Most—but not all—other teams saw the value and borrowed Veeck's idea. Coincidentally or not, the American Football League, which would kick off just a few months later, chose to do the same.

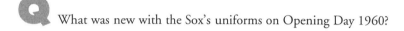

Name the Sox's four Gold Glove winners in 1960.

Minnie Minoso in left field, Jim Landis in center, Luis Aparicio at shortstop, and Nellie Fox at second base.

Q He had been the darling of Jewish-American baseball fans during his long career with the Detroit Tigers. Veeck chose him to run the Indians' farm system and then as general manager. When Veeck bought the Sox, he brought this man over as part-owner and GM. Who was he?

A Hank Greenberg. After the two sold their share of the team in 1961, they tried to get control of the new American League expansion franchise, the Los Angeles Angels. But Dodgers owner Walter O'Malley had no intention of competing against a team owned by a master promoter such as Veeck. The deal was scuttled. Greenberg, whom Jackie Robinson called one of the classiest major league players, got out of baseball and became a successful investment banker.

Q Jim Landis was often described as a great-field, no-hit member of the Go-Go Sox. Does that assessment do him an injustice?

A Perhaps not. First of all, it is true that Landis was a ballhawk in center. But he also averaged 82 runs, 64 RBIs, and 20 stolen bases between 1958 and 1962. If his numbers did not compare with those of Mickey Mantle, Willie Mays, or Duke Snider, they were better than most other center fielders of his era.

Q This native of Puerto Rico broke in with the Milwaukee Braves in 1957 and promptly helped them beat New York in the World Series. In six years (1961–1966) with the Sox, he won 69 games. Name him.

A Juan Pizarro, who pitched two no-hitters for Chicago in 1962.

Q Dave DeBusschere graduated from the University of Detroit and had a 12-year career in the National Basketball Association, winning two championships with the New York Knicks. After retirement, he served for a while as commissioner of the rival American Basketball Association. What connection did he have with the Chicago White Sox?

A He pitched for Chicago in 1962 and 1963. He is one of just 12 men to have played major league baseball and in the NBA. DeBusschere pitched in 36 games and had a 3-4 record with a 2.90 ERA. He threw 102 innings and recorded 61 strikeouts. Not bad numbers for a basketball player. But as a batter, he was atrocious—coming to the plate 22 times and getting just one hit.

Q Nellie Fox was 5' 9" and weighed 160 pounds. Did he have any power at the plate?

A Not much. He only hit 35 home runs in his long career, but he had a good eye, was handy with the bat, and could run. Not many pitchers fooled Fox, who whiffed just 216 times (once every 43 at-bats—the third-best percentage in major league history). Fox, who always played with a big wad of tobacco in his cheek, finished with 2,663 hits, 355 doubles, and 112 triples. From 1956 to 1960, he played in 798 straight games, a record for second basemen; his streak ended only because he was hospitalized with a virus.

Q Where did Fox end his career?

A He spent the 1964 and 1965 seasons in Houston, with the Colt .45s/Astros. While there, he passed much valuable knowledge to a young Joe Morgan.

Q In the trade that sent Luis Aparicio to Baltimore, he was just a throw-in. But he proved quite helpful to the 1963 White Sox, almost winning the rookie of the year award. Name this son of former pro hockey star Jimmy Ward.

A Pete Ward. On Opening Day 1963, he beat the Tigers with a seventh-inning home run—starting an 18-game hitting streak. In that season, Ward hit .295 and had 22 homers, drove in 84 runs, and scored 80 himself. In the mid-1960s, he was the White Sox' most consistent power threat in spacious Comiskey Park. Ward, a third baseman, had good range and a strong but inaccurate arm.

Q Hoyt Wilhelm, master of the knuckleball, played for nine teams in his career, the ChiSox (1963–1968) being one of them. What had he done in his first major league game, with the New York Giants, back in 1952?

A He hit a home run in his first at-bat, and he would never hit another.

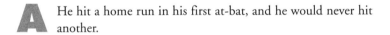

Q Who is the White Sox's one-season strikeout king?

A Dave Nicholson, whose 175 whiffs in 1963 set a major league record that has since been broken. Nicholson, who had signed with the Orioles for a $100,000 bonus in 1958, was part of the trade that sent Luis Aparicio to Baltimore. He could hit with power, but he struck out once every 2.48 at-bats. On June 12, 1963, he struck out seven times in a doubleheader against the Angels.

This native Chicagoan could be seen in the White Sox' spring training camps in 1962 and '63, but he was put on waivers and picked up by Detroit. Who was he?

Denny McLain, who would win 31 games for the 1968 Tigers.

By what means did Wilhelm get to Chicago?

He was traded from Baltimore in the deal that sent Luis Aparicio to the Orioles. Every season from 1964 to 1968, his ERA was south of 2.00, including a pretty 1.31 in 1967. Wilhelm, always frequently used, worked in 361 games in six seasons with the Sox. A fine defensive player, he set a major league record for pitchers in 1968 when he appeared in his 319th straight game without an error. The knuckleball put little strain on his arm, so he could go and go—all the way past his 49th birthday before retiring. Wilhelm had appeared in more games (1,070) than any pitcher in major league history, with a late-starting ML career that still spanned 21 years. It would have been more, but he fought in World War II— Wilhelm was at the Battle of the Bulge—and labored in the minor leagues for six years before reaching the bigs.

General manager Ed Short dealt "Little Looie" Aparicio to the Orioles prior to the 1963 season, risking the ire of many Sox fans. What did the slick-fielding Venezuelan say when he heard the news?

A bitter Aparicio predicted the White Sox would not win another pennant for 40 years; it turns out that he was quite the soothsayer. Aparicio helped the Orioles win the 1966 World Series and was back in Chicago in 1968. He finished his 18-year career with Boston.

Q The White Sox unveiled new road uniforms in 1964. What was the new look?

A The unis were powder-blue, with "Chicago" in block letters emblazoned across the chest. They replaced the grays the team had worn away from Comiskey Park since 1932. They went back to gray road uniforms in 1969.

Q Earl Battey backed up Sherman Lollar as the Sox' catcher in the late 1950s. Did he ever become a regular?

A Oh yes. Battey was a four-time All-Star with the Minnesota Twins and helped them win the 1965 AL pennant. He also won the Gold Glove four times.

Q What pitcher, a native of Terre Haute, Indiana, underwent revolutionary surgery that allowed him to keep going for another 14 seasons?

A Tommy John. He was with six different teams in a 26-year career—including the White Sox from 1965 to 1971. In 1974, while with the Los Angeles Dodgers, he permanently damaged the ulnar collateral ligament in his pitching arm (he was a southpaw). Dr. Frank Jobe replaced that ligament with a tendon from John's right arm. After a year in rehab, John came back and found that he could pitch even better than before. This opened up a brave new world in which the term "Tommy John surgery" has entered the lexicon.

Q Identify the 1966 AL rookie of the year.

A Tommy Agee, who was considered a rookie even though he had played parts of the 1962, 1963, and 1964 seasons with Cleveland, and part of '65 with Chicago. This native of Magnolia, Alabama, batted .273, hit 22 homers, and led AL outfielders in putouts. Agee was traded to the Mets two years later and helped them defeat Baltimore to win the 1969 World Series.

Q Who was "the Brat"?

A Eddie Stanky, manager of the White Sox from 1966 to mid-1968. In an 11-year playing career with the Cubs, Dodgers, Braves, Giants, and Cardinals, Stanky was known for his ability to draw walks and irritate his opponents. Stanky had managerial experience (three years with the Cards) before getting the Sox job.

Q What did Stanky do after getting canned by the White Sox?

A He was head coach at the University of South Alabama for nearly a decade before returning to the majors in 1977 with the Texas Rangers. He won his debut game, decided his heart wasn't in it, and resigned.

Q This catcher, a native of North Carolina, had an 18-year big league career that concluded with three seasons with the ChiSox from 1965 to 1967. Who was he?

A Smoky Burgess, one of the best pinch-hitters the game has ever seen. Upon his retirement, he had what was then a major league record of 145 pinch hits.

Q Who said, "There is no more beautiful sight in the world than a ballpark full of people"?

A Bill Veeck, and he was speaking of Comiskey Park. On its best days, with standing-room-only crowds, the mostly enclosed stands seemed to capture noise and make it reverberate. As one Chicago sportswriter remarked of the city's two baseball facilities, "Wrigley Field yayed, but Comiskey Park roared."

Q Don Buford came out of Linden, Texas, played football and baseball at Southern Cal, and earned a spot on the White Sox roster in 1963. An excellent leadoff batter, he split time between second and third base. What did he do after getting traded to Baltimore in 1967?

A Buford had five years with the Orioles, but he was moved to the outfield. He played in three World Series, one of which his team won. Buford concluded his career with four seasons in Japan, where he was quite popular with the fans.

Q How did Buford—then with the O's—do against Chicago on August 26, 1971?

A He struck out five times, but Baltimore overcame his ineptness at the plate with an 8-7 victory.

Q He was born in San Antonio, went to Oklahoma State University, and signed a free-agent contract with the Sox in 1959. Who was this right-handed pitcher?

A Joel Horlen. He had many fine years, but his best came in 1967 when he had a 19-7 record, 6 shutouts, and a 2.06 ERA. All of those figures were the league's best—Horlen also threw a no-hitter against the Tigers—but Jim Lonborg of Boston won the Cy Young Award. In 1972, Horlen would earn a World Series ring with the Oakland A's.

Q What did first baseman Tommie McCraw do on May 24, 1967?

A In a road game against the Twins, he hit three home runs and sent a Jim Kaat fastball to the warning track. McCraw, highly heralded as a rookie, struggled at the plate for most of his career with the White Sox. Although he was a solid defensive player, he managed to commit three errors in one inning of a game in 1968. McCraw later spent time with the Senators, Angels, and Indians.

Q Walt Williams, a member of the White Sox from 1967 to 1972 (he also played for the Colt .45s, Indians, and Yankees), was a fine outfielder, committing just 19 errors in 565 games. He was also a tough man to strike out, fanning only once every 14.3 times up. What was Williams' nickname?

A "No Neck."

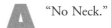

Q Who formed the all-White Sox battery for the 1968 All-Star Game in Houston?

A Pitcher Tommy John and catcher Duane Josephson.

Q Who would have thought that a portly, cigar-smoking lefthander would go on to have a series of utterly dominating seasons for the Sox? Name this native of Belmont, Massachusetts.

A Wilbur Wood. Over five seasons with the Red Sox and Pirates, he had career numbers of 1-8 with a 4.16 ERA. But the White Sox signed him and put him under the tutelage of teammate and future Hall of Famer Hoyt Wilhelm. Although Wood had thrown the knuckleball off and on since his days as a schoolboy, he did not trust it in the clutch. But Wood, with encouragement from his wife, and tips and guidance from Wilhelm, mastered the pitch. He had four seasons (1967–1970) in the ChiSox bullpen, appearing in an AL-record 88 games in 1968.

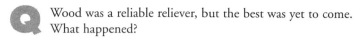

Q Wood was a reliable reliever, but the best was yet to come. What happened?

A He became a starter after Joel Horlen suffered an injury early in the 1971 season. Wood responded with a 22-13 record, tossing 334 innings and completing 22 games—two more than all of Chicago's starters had in 1970. Quickly turning himself into the ace of the staff, he took the mound 13 times that year with just two days' rest. Wood was even better in 1972, winning 24 games and throwing 388 innings (most in the majors since 1917) and starting 49 times (more than any White Sox pitcher since 1908). With the advent of the designated hitter in 1973, some baseball aficionados predicted Woods would win 30 or even 40, but he managed "just" 24 for a fairly bad ChiSox team. His career effectively ended on May 9, 1976, in Detroit when he was hit on the left knee by a drive off the bat of the Tigers' Ron LeFlore. Wood pitched ineffectually for two more years before retiring.

Q What was Williams' best day at the plate?

A It may have been at Fenway Park against the Red Sox on May 31, 1970. Williams stroked four singles and a double, scored five runs, and had two RBIs as the White Sox won, 22-13.

Q The White Sox were a franchise in trouble in the late 1960s, as average attendance dipped below 10,000. What was done in a futile effort to change things?

A In 1968 and 1969, a few home games were played in Milwaukee's County Stadium. This only fueled speculation that the team would soon be moving there.

Q What was new at Comiskey Park on Opening Day 1969?

A Artificial turf in the infield. It would be replaced with natural grass seven years later.

Q Identify Paul Edmondson in White Sox history.

A This promising right-handed pitcher won his major league debut on June 20, 1969, going the distance in a 9-1 defeat of Anaheim. He also got two hits and scored twice that day. Eight months later, Edmondson was killed in a car wreck in Santa Barbara, California.

Q What manager, a person of unrelenting optimism, was with the Sox from 1970 to 1975?

A Chuck Tanner, whose record was 401-414. He later reached the pinnacle of his profession as skipper of the 1979 World Series champion Pittsburgh Pirates.

Q How many fans were at Comiskey Park on September 25, 1970, to see Aparicio play his 2,219th game at shortstop, breaking the team mark set by Luke Appling between 1930 and 1950?

A Barely 2,000.

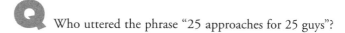

Q Who uttered the phrase "25 approaches for 25 guys"?

A Tanner, and that was how he went about managing. It was an unconventional, low-key approach, one that got maximum production from a talented-yet-temperamental player like Dick Allen, but it could go wrong too. He was at the helm in Pittsburgh in the early 1980s when the Bucs' clubhouse was suffused with marijuana and cocaine.

Q This Pennsylvania native integrated the minor league team in Little Rock, Arkansas, and became NL rookie of the year with the Phillies in 1964. He had brief stints in St. Louis and LA before arriving at what was then a moribund Comiskey Park. Identify him.

A Dick Allen, one of the top power hitters in the late 1960s and early 1970s, when pitching dominated. He put together a superb season in 1972 (.308, 37 homers, 113 RBIs) and earned MVP honors. Still, Allen's mercurial personality led to a number of suspensions, fights, and disputes. His often disinterested defensive play— primarily at third base and later at first—caused him to commit a multitude of errors. Allen's swing-from-the-heels batting style caused him to be equally prolific in strikeouts; when he retired in 1977, he had whiffed 1,556 times, fifth on the all-time list.

Q In February 1973, the White Sox gave Allen a three-year deal that made him the highest-paid player in major league history. What was his salary?

A $250,000.

Q Who was Hank Allen?

A The older and far-less-talented brother of Dick Allen. He was a utility infielder who got into 37 games with Chicago in 1972 and '73.

Q On June 4, 1972, in the second game of a doubleheader at Comiskey Park, the Yankees were ahead by two runs in the bottom of the ninth. Two men were on base. Reliever Sparky Lyle needed just one more out to win the game. Did he get it?

A No. Dick Allen, pinch-hitting for a teammate, sent Lyle's pitch into the left field upper deck for a dramatic 5-4 victory.

Q Where had Harry Caray come from?

A He was raised in the same St. Louis neighborhood that produced Yogi Berra and Joe Garagiola. Caray was 34 when he was hired to do the Cardinals' broadcasts, and he had that job for nearly a quarter-century. Fired for allegedly having a clandestine romance with the daughter of a team executive, he spent one season with the Oakland A's before getting canned by Charlie Finley. The blustery man with the Coke-bottle glasses then joined the White Sox for 11 seasons. During this time, he began singing "Take Me Out to the Ballgame" during the seventh-inning stretch and calling day games from Comiskey Park's bleachers on hot summer days. In 1982, he moved over to the Cubs organization and his popularity grew even further. Caray died in 1998, while preparing for his 54th season as a broadcaster.

Q Only two White Sox have ever led the AL in home runs. Identify them.

A Bill Melton hit 33 in 1971, and his teammate Dick Allen did it twice: 37 in 1972 and 32 in 1974.

Q Seven weeks later in Minnesota, what rarity did Allen perform?

A He became the first major league player since 1950 to hit two inside-the-park homers in a game. The Twins' Bert Blyleven was the victim both times. The Sox won, 8-1.

Q This pitcher was AL rookie of the year with the Yankees in 1968 and got shipped to Chicago in December 1971 in a straight-up swap for Rich McKinney. Who was he?

A Stan Bahnsen. He won 21 games in 1972, although he set what was then a major league record by being taken out in 36 of his 41 starts. In a game against the Indians in 1973, he had a no-hitter with two outs in the ninth when Walt Williams singled over a drawn-in infield. Bahnsen, who was often irked by the criticism of announcer Harry Caray, who chided him for lackadaisical play, was dealt to Oakland in mid-1975.

Q What big league mark did Ed Herrmann tie on July 4, 1972?

A He was the third catcher ever to have three double plays in a nine-inning game in the Sox' 2-1 defeat of the Orioles before 26,105 fans at Comiskey Park. Herrmann did this by throwing out three would-be stealers following strikeouts.

Q Jorge Orta made his debut with the White Sox in 1972. He was primarily a second baseman, but he also played in the outfield and DH'ed. A steady player for Chicago for most of a decade, Orta would help the Kansas City Royals capture a title in 1985. But outside of the U.S., what was his main claim to fame?

A His father, Pedro Orta, one of the greats of Cuban baseball.

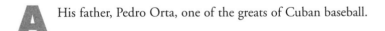

Q Hard-throwing Rich "Goose" Gossage was with the Sox the first five years (1972–1976) of his long career, which would include 310 saves and 115 relief victories—third best in that category behind Hoyt Wilhelm and Lindy McDaniel. After manager Paul Richards made him a starter in 1976, he had a woeful 9-17 record and was sent to the Pirates. Who did Chicago get in return?

A Gossage was traded, along with Terry Forster, for Silvio Martinez and Richie Zisk.

Q What was the largest crowd ever to witness a baseball game at Comiskey Park?

A On May 20, 1973, no fewer than 55,555 fans gathered to see the Sox and Twins play a doubleheader.

Q And the smallest?

A On May 6, 1971, just 511 souls showed up for a game between the White Sox and the Red Sox.

Q Who were the principals in a struggle for control of Chicago's clubhouse in 1974?

A Dick Allen and Ron Santo. Santo had been with the crosstown Cubs for 14 years. While there, he hit more than 300 home runs, won five Gold Gloves, and was a nine-time All-Star. So, Santo definitely had credentials. He came to the Sox in an off-season trade, initiating a bitter, yearlong battle between him and Allen. The two had a personality conflict from the start and at least one physical clash. In essence, Allen had a quieter approach to the matter of leadership, whereas Santo was gung-ho and confrontational. The team, once expected to contend for a pennant, limped home with a .500 record. It was the last year of Santo's career, although he has a great many admirers—not only for his achievements with the Cubs but as an athlete who has dealt with diabetes most of his life. Both of Santo's legs have been amputated as a result, but he continues to work as a radio announcer for the Cubs.

Q This pitcher, a native of Zeeland, Michigan, had a 25-year career. During that time, he won the Gold Glove 16 straight times. Who was he? Hint: His nickname was "Kitty."

A Jim Kaat, who was with the Sox in 1974 and 1975, winning 41 games.

Q What former Chicago player died in Red Bluff, California, on October 13, 1975?

A Swede Risberg, last of the infamous "eight men out" from the Black Sox scandal. After his exile, Risberg had played semi-pro ball, worked on a dairy farm, and ran a saloon that bore his name.

Q What fashion faux pas did Veeck instigate for the first game of a doubleheader against Kansas City on April 8, 1976?

A He equipped his team with short pants. The Sox players were embarrassed to wear them, and the Royals could barely contain their laughter.

Q What was Veeck's bright idea on July 3, 1976, when Chicago lost to the Rangers, 3-0?

A It was the first morning game in Comiskey Park history, drawing just over 10,000 fans despite a tie-in with a national fast-food chain that gave out free breakfasts. The first pitch was thrown at 10:30 a.m.

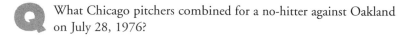 What Chicago pitchers combined for a no-hitter against Oakland on July 28, 1976?

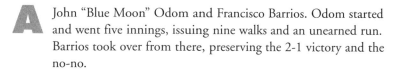 John "Blue Moon" Odom and Francisco Barrios. Odom started and went five innings, issuing nine walks and an unearned run. Barrios took over from there, preserving the 2-1 victory and the no-no.

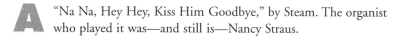 What song with a catchy chorus began to be used at Comiskey Park in 1977 as a multi-purpose anthem for either home runs or a change in opposing pitchers?

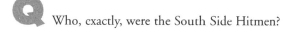 "Na Na, Hey Hey, Kiss Him Goodbye," by Steam. The organist who played it was—and still is—Nancy Straus.

Who, exactly, were the South Side Hitmen?

They were the 1977 Chicago White Sox, a team that was not adept at catching, running, or throwing. Nor did they pitch well. Some had been unwanted and unloved by other teams in the past. But these very qualities made them one of the most entertaining teams in Sox history. Bunt to move runners along? No. Steal bases to distract the opposing defense? Oh, please! Turn the double play? Why bother? They just whacked the ball—long, hard, and often. They finished third in the AL West behind Kansas City and Texas, but they won 90 games (26 more than the '76 club) and were big-time draws at the ticket box. Oscar Gamble, Richie Zisk, and Eric Soderholm were new acquisitions, leading Chicago to a franchise-record 192 home runs. In 1977, at least, the Sox were first in the hearts of baseball fans across the city, not just on the South Side.

Q This outfielder had a 17-year career (1969–1985) with seven different teams—the Cubs, Phillies, Indians, Yankees (twice), White Sox (twice), Padres, and Rangers. Who was he? Hint: He wore a famously big Afro.

A Oscar Gamble, who hit 31 homers for the Sox in 1977. He was a perfect example of Bill Veeck's "rent-a-player" philosophy. Veeck lacked the money to compete for talented players and resorted to quick-fix trades—for instance, the time he got Gamble, two minor leaguers, and cash from the Yankees in exchange for Bucky Dent. Gamble had a superb season and then left for San Diego and the riches of free agency.

Q This native of Jackson, Mississippi, a member of the White Sox from 1975 to 1981, was one of the few stars Veeck could afford to keep. Who was he?

A Chet Lemon, who hit 44 doubles in 1979 to lead the AL. He was traded to the Tigers in 1982 and in two years was celebrating a World Series title.

Q Who was the first female television play-by-play announcer in major league history?

A In 1977, the White Sox hired 28-year-old Mary Shane for that post. She teamed with Harry Caray, Jimmy Piersall, and Lorn Brown in the WSNS booth for one season.

Q Don Kessinger is best known for his fine defensive play for the Cubs over an 11-year span. What did he do with the ChiSox?

A Kessinger, who graduated from the University of Mississippi, joined the Sox in late 1977. He was the team's player/manager in 1979, but things were not going well and he got canned before the season ended. Kessinger never played or managed again.

Q Who hit the Sox' first indoor home run?

A On July 4, 1977, Oscar Gamble hit one into the seats in Chicago's 6-2 defeat of the Mariners at the Seattle Kingdome.

Q Kevin Hickey, a left-handed reliever with a herky-jerky motion, grew up in the Windy City and played three years each with the Sox and Orioles. How did his pro baseball career get started?

A In 1977, Hickey was a softball pitcher signed after one of the White Sox' public tryouts.

Q Who was the winning pitcher on June 7, 1978, when the Sox beat the Twins for the 6,000th victory in franchise history?

A Ken Kravec.

Q What pitcher was with the White Sox from 1978 to 1982, went across town and helped the Cubbies reach the post-season for the first time in 39 years? Hint: His nickname was "Rainbow."

A Steve Trout, son of former Tigers pitching star Dizzy Trout. The nickname was a fairly obvious takeoff of his "fishy" last name, but it also fit with his distinct, offbeat personality. Trout, who later played with the Yankees and Mariners, could shut a team down or be miserably erratic. This, too, contributed to his reputation as a flake.

Q From 1972 to 1979, relief pitcher Ron Schueler had a 40-48 record with four teams—the last of which was the White Sox. How did his playing career come to an end?

A In June 1979, pitching coach Freddie Martin died. Schueler, who was just 31 years old at the time, retired as a player and took Martin's place. He would coach in Chicago and elsewhere before returning in 1991 as general manager. During his decade in that job, the Sox won three division titles: 1993, 1994, and 2000.

Q Outfielder Ralph Garr was with the Sox in the late 1970s, but his career is best remembered for something he did while playing for the Atlanta Braves. What was it?

A In 1974, he had 149 hits entering the All-Star break—a record that still stands. Garr, it should be noted, cooled off a bit in the second half of the season but still finished with 214 hits.

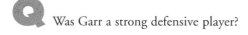 Was Garr a strong defensive player?

No; anything hit his way was an adventure not to be missed. Garr made 76 errors in his career, and that number would be higher if he had not played so cautiously.

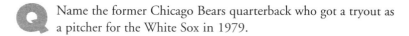 Name the former Chicago Bears quarterback who got a tryout as a pitcher for the White Sox in 1979.

Bobby Douglass. Needless to say, he did not make the team.

 Who was responsible for Disco Demolition Night?

Mike Veeck, son of the White Sox' owner, deserves most of the credit (or blame, as the case may be). This ill-conceived promotional stunt took place on July 12, 1979, at Comiskey Park. It was held during a scheduled twilight doubleheader between the Sox and the Detroit Tigers. With the involvement of a local radio DJ who disliked that particular musical art form, the event turned into mayhem and was the worst idea since the Cleveland Indians' infamous Ten Cent Beer Night in 1974. Those who brought unwanted disco records to the game were admitted for 98 cents. Veeck had hoped to bring in an extra 5,000 fans, but 50,000 passed through the turnstiles with thousands more outside clamoring to get in. The TV announcers noted the many "strange people" wandering aimlessly in the stands, and the pregame air was heavy with the scent of marijuana. Records were used as Frisbees, beer was thrown, and firecrackers were lit.

Q When did it really get out of hand?

A In between games, there was supposed to be a symbolic destruction of disco music in center field. A bomb was detonated and ripped a hole in the outfield grass surface as thousands of people ran onto the field, starting their own fires and engaging in mini-riots. They wrecked the batting cage and stole the bases. PA announcer Harry Caray implored them to leave the field immediately, but to no avail. Eventually, police in riot gear were called in. There were six injuries and 39 arrests. Tigers manager Sparky Anderson refused to send his team out for the second game, which was forfeited to Detroit. The field at Comiskey Park showed signs of destruction for the rest of the '79 season.

Q Tony La Russa was named the White Sox' manager midway through the 1979 season. What was his baseball background?

A La Russa, who came from Tampa, was a promising middle infielder in the early 1960s. But a shoulder injury in his rookie year never quite healed. He played a total of 132 major league games with the A's, Braves, and Cubs. His numbers were modest: .199 batting average, 7 RBIs, and 15 runs scored. He earned a law degree from Florida State before Chicago tabbed him in '79. He was named American League manager of the year in 1983 when his club won the AL West, but he was fired after a slow start in 1986. La Russa went on to 10 years in Oakland and recently finished his 11th season with the Cards. Only the second manager to win championships in both leagues, he currently trails only Connie Mack and John McGraw on the all-time managerial wins list.

Q Wayne Nordhagen had an eight-year (1976–1983) career, most of that time being spent with the White Sox. What did he do in 1979 that was fairly unique in big league history?

A He served as both a pitcher and a catcher. He was on the mound for two innings in two different games and had a 9.00 ERA.

Q Identify Andrew Rozdilsky, Jr.

A That's Andy the Clown, who performed, quite unofficially, in the stands at White Sox home games from 1960 to 1990. A Chicago native, he was invited to a game by some friends and decided to attend dressed in a clown costume; to his delight, the crowd responded well and he was soon performing at all home games. Rather prominent in his bowler hat, black-rimmed glasses, polka-dot costume, and bulbous red nose, he cheered the Sox often and loudly. Andy the Clown may have been the last in a generation of clowns who appeared regularly at major league games—others being Al Schacht, Max Patkin, and Emmett Kelly. He predated the San Diego Chicken, the Phillie Phanatic, and others of their ilk. In 1981, the White Sox' new owners, Jerry Reinsdorf and Eddie Einhorn, tried to get rid of him and faced such strong opposition that they changed their minds after just one day. Once New Comiskey Park opened in 1991, however, it was made clear that Andy the Clown's 30-year reign had come to an end. Rozdilsky died in 1995.

Q Which managers have won the most games in a Sox uniform?

A Jimmy Dykes (899), Al Lopez (840), Tony La Russa (522), Jerry Manuel (500), and Fielder Jones (426).

Q What did the White Sox' Mike Squires do on May 4, 1980, that was so unusual?

A He caught the final inning of an 11–1 loss to the Brewers, becoming the first left-hander to catch in the major leagues since Dale Long in 1958. Three years later, Squires became the first left-handed third baseman in at least 50 years.

Q How did Carlton Fisk become a member of the Chicago White Sox after the 1980 season?

A The Red Sox' front office blundered by failing to postmark Fisk's new contract in time, which allowed him to become a free agent. Changing the color of his Sox, Fisk also switched his uniform number from 27 to 72. As fate would have it, the 1981 season began at Fenway Park and Fisk hit a three-run, eighth-inning homer to win the game for his new team.

Q This starting pitcher came from South Carolina and won his first nine decisions, tying a club record first set by Lefty Williams in 1917. He had pinpoint control on the mound and not much at all off the mound. Identify him.

A LaMarr Hoyt. In 1982, he led the American League with 19 wins and walked just 48 batters in 239 innings. He had a career year in 1983, winning the Cy Young Award and pacing the White Sox to the American League West title with a 24-10 record and 3.66 ERA. This time, Hoyt surrendered just 31 walks in 260 innings. He beat the Orioles in the first game of the 1983 ALCS, but the White Sox lost the series and would not be back in the playoffs for another 10 years.

Q He had been a member of the Dodgers organization, but a spinal fusion in 1978 seemed to end his baseball dreams. Back home in Gary, Indiana, he was working in construction when he got an invitation to a tryout at Comiskey Park. His dreams were revived and fulfilled when he hit 35 home runs, played in the All-Star Game, was named 1983 rookie of the year, and helped his team reach the post-season for the first time since 1959. To whom do we refer?

A Ron Kittle, whose 150 strikeouts that year led the American League. Later hampered by injuries, he played for the Yankees, Indians, Orioles, and the Sox twice more before quitting in 1991.

Q Under what circumstances did Tom Paciorek join the White Sox?

A Paciorek, a two-sport (baseball and football) athlete at the University of Houston, had just finished the best season of his 18-year major league career. He batted .326 for Seattle and made an appearance in the All-Star Game in 1981, but the Mariners chose to ship him to Chicago. Paciorek, an outfielder/first baseman, was with the Sox for three years. His brothers, John and Jim, also reached the major leagues, with Houston and Milwaukee, respectively.

Q What designated hitter, who was known as "the Bull," hit three home runs onto the roof at Comiskey Park?

A Greg Luzinski, who connected all three times off Dennis "Oil Can" Boyd of the Red Sox in a 6-2 Chicago victory. The next season, he would be just the 10th player in major league history to hit grand slams in consecutive games. A clumsy if not wretched left fielder in his earlier days with the Phillies, Luzinski was strictly a DH in his four seasons (1981–1984) with the Sox.

Q He was college player of the year at Arizona State in 1976, and the Astros chose him with the first pick in the draft. He didn't last long in Houston or in Seattle, but his 90-mph fastball, sharp slider, and excellent curveball enticed the Sox, who acquired him in 1983. Who was he?

A Floyd Bannister, a man who played a big role in Chicago's 1983 division title. He went 13-1 with a 2.23 ERA after the All-Star break. But baseball observers thought Bannister lacked the killer instinct and was unwilling to pitch inside; thus he gave up lots of long balls. After winning 16 games in 1987, he was traded by the White Sox to the Royals for four prospects.

Q The 1982 White Sox had won 87 games, and hopes were high for further improvement in '83. They were five games under .500 and languishing in fifth place in mid-June. What trade by GM Roland Hemond is credited with turning the season around?

A He sent second baseman Tony Bernazard to Seattle in exchange for his counterpart, Julio Cruz. The team was three games over .500 by the All-Star break and played nearly .700 ball the rest of the way.

Q Not everyone was impressed, however. What opposing manager insisted the bubble would soon burst?

A Doug Rader of the Texas Rangers, who said, "They're not playing that well. They're winning ugly." Thus was born a rallying cry. On September 17, 1983, the White Sox clinched Chicago's first championship since the Bears won the NFL title in 1963. The Sox came into October with a 20-game bulge over second-place Kansas City—and 22 over Rader's Rangers.

Q This big lefty, a native of Houston, made his White Sox debut at age 19. With a 15-13 record and 2.84 ERA in 1980, he was off to a good start. Who was he?

A Britt Burns, who would go on to pitch 30 straight scoreless innings in 1981. Burns threw valiantly in the last game of the 1983 ALCS, holding the Orioles in check for nine innings before losing. His career ended due to a chronic, degenerative hip condition.

Q Soon after taking over, new owners Jerry Reinsdorf and Eddie Einhorn embarked on an ambitious renovation of Comiskey Park. Of what did it consist?

A More luxury boxes were added in the upper deck, the bullpens were moved into a now-shrunken center field, and the diamond was moved toward the outfield (which, of course, meant the action was that much farther away from fans behind home plate). There was a new press box and a big new scoreboard. Reinsdorf and Einhorn spent millions on long-deferred maintenance and infrastructure improvements. The stadium had not looked so good in a long, long time. Barely five years later, though, the battle to replace aging Comiskey Park began and climaxed with the passing of new stadium funding legislation in 1988. The White Sox played their last game there two years later. For the oldest ballpark in the major leagues, the rebirth proved to be fleeting.

Q This man was pitching for the Mexico City Diablos Rojos (Red Devils) during the 1981 major league players' strike. The Sox signed him, and he saved 21 games the next year. Identify him.

A Salome Barojas.

Q He stole 40 bases as a rookie with the Los Angeles Dodgers in 1980, had trouble hitting, and was sent to the minors the next year. Chicago picked him up in 1982, and he became the team's leadoff man. Identify this native of Waco, Texas.

A Rudy Law. He was a catalyst for the 1983 division champions, led AL outfielders in fielding percentage, and broke Luis Aparicio's club stolen-base record (77). Law gave up his jersey number, 11, in 1984 when it was retired in honor of Aparicio.

Q Carlton Fisk defied the aging process in Chicago, occasionally playing in the outfield, at first base, or as a DH, but most of his games were behind the plate. His steady play helped the White Sox to the 1983 AL West title. How did he do in the ALCS against Baltimore?

A He batted just .176 as Chicago fell to the O's in four games.

Q Tom Seaver won two games for the White Sox on May 9, 1984. How was this possible?

A Chicago and Milwaukee had played 17 innings the day before, and the game was suspended with the score tied at 3. The teams returned to Comiskey Park the next day and played eight more innings. It did not end until Harold Baines homered off Chuck Porter for a 7-6 win in the longest game in AL history: 25 innings and more than 8 hours. Seaver pitched the final inning and then started and won the regularly scheduled game.

Q General manager Roland Hemond was roundly criticized for orchestrating a seven-player deal in 1984 with San Diego—in fact, he was fired soon thereafter. The trade sent Cy Young Award winner LaMarr Hoyt to the Padres. Who was one of the prospects Chicago got in return?

A Ozzie Guillen, a shortstop who went on to become AL rookie of the year in '85. He committed just 12 errors that year and batted a surprising .273. Guillen's bubbly and brash attitude was initially seen by some as hot-dogging, but his critics soon vanished. His leadership in the clubhouse and on the field was undeniable.

Q Guillen, a native of Venezuela, was soon compared with what former Chicago player who hailed from there?

A Luis Aparicio, who had been compared with fellow *venezolano* Chico Carrasquel. Guillen's speed and range allowed him to make acrobatic plays at short, although he sometimes displayed dubious judgment at the plate, swinging at balls over his head or in the dirt. By walking just 10 times in 150 games in 1996, Guillen set a major league record. Despite that and a series of injuries, his popularity and style kept him afloat as he moved to Baltimore, Atlanta, and Tampa Bay. His playing career lasted 16 years. Guillen's ex-teammate, Kenny Williams, hired him as the White Sox' manager in November 2003.

Q What brilliant but erratic pitcher threw a no-hitter against the Angels on September 19, 1986?

A Joe Cowley. In that 7-1 victory, he walked seven and struck out eight.

Q On July 18, 1984, the Sox made a trade with the Yankees, giving up two players to be named later for shortstop Roy Smalley. Good trade or bad trade?

A Bad trade. Smalley did little in 47 games and was soon dealt to the Twins. Meanwhile, one of those anonymous players who were sent to the Bronx was Doug Drabek, a future Cy Young Award winner.

Q In 1984, average attendance at home games was about 26,000. It declined steadily each of the next five years to less than half that. There were rumors of the club moving to St. Petersburg or Orlando. What fueled them?

A The team ran a weekend promotion that featured players posing with Mickey Mouse and his sidekicks.

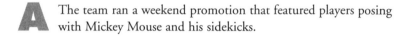

Q There were many reasons the Sox faltered in 1984, and LaMarr Hoyt was one of them. He went 13-18 and had a 4.47 ERA—a fairly alarming drop. How did things go for him after being traded to San Diego?

A He made the 1985 NL All-Star team and was the game's MVP. After the season, though, Hoyt was arrested twice within a month on drug possession charges. He had a desultory 1986 season, got busted again, and was barred from baseball by Commissioner Peter Ueberroth. When the Padres released Hoyt—and after a 45-day prison stint—the Sox gave him a second chance but he never made it back to the major leagues. Hoyt was 31 when his once-promising career ended.

Q He won 311 games in his 20-season career, 31 of which came with the Sox in 1984 and '85. Of what Hall of Fame pitcher do we refer?

A Tom Seaver, the 1967 NL rookie of the year with the Mets and three-time Cy Young Award winner. He holds the record for giving up the most roof-shot home runs (four) at old Comiskey Park.

Q Catcher Ron Hassey was traded no fewer than four times between the White Sox and the Yankees in 1984 and 1985. For what is he best known?

A He is the only player in major league history to catch two perfect games. Hassey was behind the plate with Cleveland for Len Barker's masterpiece in 1981 and with Montreal 10 years later when Dennis Martinez did it.

Q How did the White Sox celebrate Comiskey Park's 75th season on July 1, 1985?

A There was a postgame concert by Alabama. Unfortunately, the Seattle Mariners spoiled the birthday by beating the Sox, 3-1.

Q He had been with the Expos, Tigers, and the Expos again before arriving in Chicago in 1985 and earning a club-record 32 saves. Who was this intimidating, 6' 4", 230-pound pitcher?

A Bob James. Unfortunately, he suffered an arm injury late in the 1986 season and never regained his 92-mph fastball. Released in '87, James recorded 73 career saves.

Q What right-handed pitcher became Chicago's bullpen ace in 1987 following Bob James' injury problems?

A Bobby Thigpen, who was soon engaged in a public salary dispute with the White Sox front office. Thigpen chose to state his case in doggerel verse, and the team responded in like fashion; the *Wall Street Journal* printed some of their exchanges. Thigpen proved his worth convincingly, saving 34 games in 1988.

Q Ken Harrelson had a nine-year career with Kansas City, Washington, Boston, and Cleveland before an ill-fated attempt to make it as a pro golfer. What did this South Carolina native do next?

A He was a broadcaster with the Red Sox and then the White Sox. In 1986, for reasons that mystified fans, he was hired as Chicago's general manager. That experiment lasted one year, during which time Harrelson fired manager Tony La Russa and made some trades that could only be called unwise. And yet he had enough support within the organization to go back to his old job as a play-by-play announcer.

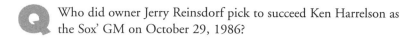

Q Who did owner Jerry Reinsdorf pick to succeed Ken Harrelson as the Sox' GM on October 29, 1986?

A Larry Himes, who built the White Sox farm system and drafted such players as Jack McDowell, Robin Ventura, Frank Thomas, and Alex Fernandez. He also traded one of the franchise's most popular players, Harold Baines, in July 1989. One of the players the Sox got from the Rangers in that deal was a skinny 20-year-old outfielder named Sammy Sosa. Himes' moves, the dugout work of manager Jeff Torborg, and strong seasons from vets like Ivan Calderon, Ozzie Guillen, Bobby Thigpen, and Carlton Fisk, enabled the White Sox to contend with eventual AL champ Oakland in 1990. Despite a 25-game improvement, Himes and his director of scouting, Al Goldis, were fired.

Q Did Himes leave Chicago?

A No. Just days after he got his pink slip, Himes was hired by the Cubs in the same capacity. Again he traded for Sosa, in exchange for George Bell. At first, this appeared to be a lopsided trade but Bell was soon out of baseball and Sosa was bulking up and busting homers right and left. The Cubbies were floundering by 1994, at which time Himes was fired again as players at Wrigley Field groaned about his draconian clubhouse rules and management style.

Q Who did the most damage in the Sox's 17-0 crushing of the Cleveland Indians on July 5, 1987?

A Kenny Williams and Harold Baines had 4 RBIs each, and Ozzie Guillen and Greg Walker had 3 each as Chicago pounded out 21 hits.

Q Who swiped an American League rookie-record 50 bases for the 1986 White Sox?

A John Cangelosi. The 5' 8" Brooklyn native, a spunky switch-hitter, moved ahead of Rudy Law and Daryl Boston to win the center-field job in spring training. Despite his rookie showing, he was dealt to Pittsburgh the very next year. Cangelosi, who bounced in and out of the majors, was with the Florida Marlins when they won the 1997 World Series.

Q What five pitchers had the most wins upon joining the White Sox?

A Steve Carlton leads the list. He had 314 victories before coming to Chicago in 1986. He is followed by Tom Seaver (273/1984), Red Ruffing (270/1947), Early Wynn (235/1958), and Chief Bender (212/1925).

Q Was 1987 a good year for pitcher Jack McDowell?

A Yes. He led Stanford to the College World Series championship, was the White Sox' top pick in the draft, won a Southern League crown with the Birmingham Barons, and joined the White Sox in September. His major league career began with 13 scoreless innings. He finished the season at 3-0 and a 1.93 ERA.

Q Did he keep up that pace?

A No. McDowell soon developed a sore arm and went down to the minors for a while. He was back with the Sox in 1990, going 14-9 with 165 strikeouts. Over the next three seasons, he was the intimidating power pitcher Chicago's fans had hoped for, with a split-fingered fastball and forkball, winning 59 games. He won the Cy Young Award in 1993, had a somewhat disappointing season the next year, made some nasty remarks about team management, and got shipped to the Yankees.

Q This veteran lefty had been a steady performer throughout the 1970s and mid-1980s for the Astros, Pirates, and Dodgers. His numbers went into a serious decline after the 1985 season. Nevertheless, he made the White Sox' club in 1988 and came through with a superb season. Who was he?

A Jerry Reuss, who had 13 wins and a 3.44 ERA, lowest among the team's starting pitchers. On May 9, he notched his 200th victory as Chicago beat Baltimore. Reuss, the team's Opening Day starter in 1989, was traded to the Brewers a few months later.

Q Name the famous tavern south of 35th Street where Babe Ruth had once gone in for a beer between games of a doubleheader.

A McCuddy's, which was razed in 1989.

Q American League MVP with Toronto in 1987, this native of the Dominican Republican hit a walk-off home run against the White Sox on May 28, 1989. Name him.

A George Bell, who had two years (1992 and 1993) in Chicago. A man with a big strike zone but a poor defensive player, he could be testy and contentious with fans, teammates, and the media.

Q What incident involving Carlton Fisk and the Yankees' Deion Sanders took place in May 1990?

A Fisk was widely admired for his work ethic and respect of the game itself. Sanders hit a pop fly and failed to run to first base, assuming that the ball would be easily caught. Fisk berated Sanders and told him during his next at-bat, "If you don't play it [the game] right, I'm going to kick your ass right here in Yankee Stadium." Sanders, an erstwhile football player, issued an apology the following day.

Q Did the Yankees' Andy Hawkins pitch well against the Sox on July 1, 1990?

A Very well, tossing a no-hitter. Unfortunately for Hawkins, the White Sox scored four unearned runs in the eighth inning and he lost, 4-0.

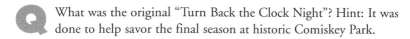

What was the original "Turn Back the Clock Night"? Hint: It was done to help savor the final season at historic Comiskey Park.

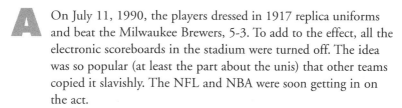

On July 11, 1990, the players dressed in 1917 replica uniforms and beat the Milwaukee Brewers, 5-3. To add to the effect, all the electronic scoreboards in the stadium were turned off. The idea was so popular (at least the part about the unis) that other teams copied it slavishly. The NFL and NBA were soon getting in on the act.

Frank Thomas, American League MVP in 1993 and 1994,
is the club's all-time leader in runs scored, home runs, doubles,
RBIs, extra-base hits, walks, and total bases.

CHAPTER FIVE

A NEW HOME
ACROSS THE STREET

Comiskey Park was showing its age. Luxury suites and a few other amenities had been added, but it remained the oldest park in major league baseball: older than Fenway Park, older than Tiger Stadium, older than Wrigley Field. Structural engineers (hired by the club) were saying that it might not last too much longer. The White Sox, now in the hands of Jerry Reinsdorf and Eddie Einhorn—who dearly wanted out of the South Side—had plans for constructing a new facility in the Chicago suburb of Addison; a 140-acre site and architectural plans were in place. But in 1988, when the voters of Addison turned down the bond resolution that would have funded the new park, Reinsdorf played hardball, issuing an ultimatum to the city of Chicago. If they did not build a new stadium, the White Sox were moving to Florida.

Reinsdorf could make this threat because St. Petersburg, Florida, had begun work on a baseball stadium in hopes of luring a team (like, maybe, the White Sox) down there. Illinois governor James Thompson advocated for the construction of a new stadium next to the current Comiskey Park. He twisted some arms in Springfield, and the deed was done. Ground was broken on May 7, 1989, for New Comiskey Park directly across the street from where the cornerstone had been set for the original 79 years earlier. It cost the relatively small sum of $167 million. Thompson threw out the first pitch on Opening Day 1991, and New Comiskey Park set a franchise attendance record of 2,934,154 that year.

The stadium had unobstructed views, a spacious clubhouse for the players, and 90 suites in which well-heeled patrons could watch games in air-conditioned splendor. Those who designed the park tried to retain some of the charm of the original (now being called Old Comiskey Park), such as its arched windows and the general look of the center field scoreboard.

Although it was new and clean, the park was sterile and the subject of considerable criticism—especially when the Baltimore Orioles' new facility opened, more successfully blending the traditional baseball feel with modern touches. The upper deck was too steep in Chicago and the seats there were too far away. Mike Veeck, son of the former White Sox owner, echoed the complaints of many fans when he said, "It has everything but a soul."

In response, the stadium has been considerably changed since its opening. Done in seven phases from 2001 to 2007, the alterations have included constructing a multi-tiered concourse in center field, shifting the fences to make the outfield less symmetrical, and removing 6,000 seats at the top of the upper deck. These changes, done at a cost of about $120 million, have wrought a major improvement to the stadium's ambience. But as Cubs fans and other critics would note, it still sits in the hardscrabble Armor Square and Bridgeport neighborhoods of south Chicago.

When was the last time a major pro sports venue was built in Chicago, prior to New Comiskey Park in 1991?

Chicago Stadium (home of the Blackhawks and later the Bulls), which was constructed in 1929.

What gut-wrenching scene was on view in the spring and summer of 1991?

The sight of bulldozers and cranes taking apart Old Comiskey Park, site of so much sports history over a span of eight decades.

Q In 1988, GM Larry Himes worked a trade with St. Louis that brought a young center fielder to the Sox organization. After struggling for a couple of years, he was in the big leagues to stay. Who was this Cincinnati native?

A Lance Johnson, who batted no lower than .274 each year between 1990 and 1994. He led the American League in triples four straight seasons and covered a lot of ground in center. Johnson was a big part of the White Sox' winning the 1993 division championship.

Q He was born in Puerto Rico, played collegiately at Vanderbilt, and spent four good years (1991–1994) at second base for the Sox. Who was he?

A Joey Cora, who was loved by the fans for his hustle, grit, and good nature. He has been on the team's coaching staff since 2004.

Q They called this swift left fielder "Rock," and he played for the White Sox from 1991 to 1995. He was also with the Expos, Yankees, Orioles, and Marlins in a 23-year career. Who was he?

A Tim Raines, whose career numbers include a .294 batting average, 170 home runs, 980 RBIs, 1,571 runs scored, 808 stolen bases, 430 doubles, and 113 triples. Raines could really wreak havoc on the basepaths.

Q This right fielder had back troubles while with Boston, but the White Sox took a chance on him in 1993 and it turned out very well. Who was he, and how did he do?

A The man in question is Ellis Burks, who played in 146 games and hit .275 with 17 home runs and 74 RBIs in helping the Sox win the AL West. Burks emerged as a team leader as the season wore on, and hit .304 with a homer and 3 RBIs as the Sox lost in the ALCS. He was a one-year wonder as far as ChiSox fans were concerned, moving on to the Colorado Rockies in 1994.

Q Name the two Auburn University football players who would join the White Sox in the 1990s.

A Running back Bo Jackson and tight end Frank Thomas. Jackson, winner of the 1985 Heisman Trophy, played four years with the Los Angeles Raiders of the NFL. A hip injury in 1990 ended his days on the gridiron, but he underwent surgery, rehabbed, and was able to play 23 games for the Sox the next year. Although problems with that hip kept Jackson on the sidelines in 1992, he came back to hit 16 homers and drive in 45 runs the next season. His blazing speed, however, was gone; in two years with the Sox, Jackson did not steal a single base. He was with the Angels in 1994 before retiring

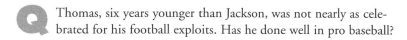

Q Thomas, six years younger than Jackson, was not nearly as celebrated for his football exploits. Has he done well in pro baseball?

A Very well indeed. Born and raised in Columbus, Georgia, he grew to 6' 5" and 240 pounds. Thomas played first base early in his career but was not especially good at it. Chicago's managers made him a full-time designated hitter after a few years. No other player in major league history has had seven straight seasons of a .300 average, 100 RBIs, 100 runs, 100 walks, and 20 home runs, which Thomas did from 1991 to 1997. This is all the more remarkable considering that the strike-shortened 1994 season limited him to 113 games. Only five players in history (Hank Aaron, Jimmie Foxx, Mel Ott, Babe Ruth, and Ted Williams) have both hit more home runs and have a higher career batting average than Thomas. On the other hand, none of them were designated hitters.

Q Thomas played 16 years with the ChiSox. How did it end?

A His numbers were undeniably going down, so the team invoked a "diminished skills" clause in his contract. In 2005, Thomas played in just 35 games although he hit 12 home runs. An injury kept him off the postseason roster when the Sox won the World Series title. Thomas' departure was somewhat unpleasant. He and White Sox general manager Kenny Williams traded barbs before Thomas left to join the Oakland A's (and then the Toronto Blue Jays). Sensitive and sometimes cantankerous, Thomas nevertheless built quite a White Sox legacy. He is the club's all-time leader in home runs (448), runs scored (1,327), RBIs (1,465), doubles (447), extra-base hits (906), walks (1,466), total bases (3,949), slugging percentage (.568), and on-base percentage (.427).

Q How did Thomas do on May 22, 2006, when the A's faced the White Sox in Chicago?

A He homered twice in his first game against his former team. When Thomas came up to lead off the second inning, a tribute to his contributions to the franchise was prepared—a musical montage on the Jumbotron at U.S. Cellular Field. The fans gave him a standing O.

Q Who was the White Sox's third-round pick in the 1982 amateur draft?

A Kenny Williams, a football and baseball player at Stanford, who is now the club's GM. He worked his way through the minor league system, reaching "the show" in 1986. A center fielder, Williams spent three years in Chicago and later played in Detroit, Toronto, and Montreal. His best year as a player was in 1987, when he batted .281 for the Sox, hit 11 home runs, and had 50 RBIs.

Q This infielder had been NL rookie of the year with the Dodgers in 1982 and played for the South Siders a decade later. Who was he?

A Steve Sax, who was five times an All-Star until he developed a case of the "yips" in which his throwing mechanics broke down; Sax had 30 errors—most of them throwing errors—in one season.

Q Any player who got cut by the Expos, as Williams was after the 1991 season, should have known that he was at the end of the line. So what did Williams do?

A He rejoined the White Sox organization as a scout, found favor with Reinsdorf, and became his special assistant. Williams did some work in the broadcast booth before becoming the team's director of minor league operations (1995), vice-president of player development (1997), and finally general manager (2000), taking over for Ron Schueler. It was he who hired Ozzie Guillen to manage the team. He took a number of aggressive actions to bolster the Sox' lineup, changing the on-field focus from home runs to pitching, defense, and speed. This was done through free agent signings, trades, and the farm system. His moves seemed to work, especially in 2005 as the Sox had the best record in the majors most of the season, won their first AL Central title in five years, their first AL pennant since 1959, and their first World Series since before the Black Sox scandal.

Q What trade was made on March 30, 1992? Hint: It was one that would live in infamy for Sox fans.

A Outfielder Sammy Sosa and pitcher Ken Patterson were sent to the Cubs in exchange for George Bell. Sosa's first full season with the Sox was 1990, but his numbers were not so hot: .233 with 15 homers. He slumped so badly in 1991 that he was shipped to the minors for awhile. But Bell, once a big home run threat in Toronto, did not get it done with the Sox and his surliness became a clubhouse distraction during the 1993 postseason. Meanwhile, Sosa became quite a bomber for the Cubs. It was painful for Sox fans to watch him and Mark McGwire battle for Roger Maris' single-season home run mark in 1998. But many baseball historians have come to view that home-run derby as somewhat bogus, since both sluggers are widely thought to have been chemically enhanced.

Q On August 4, 1993, the Rangers beat the White Sox in Arlington, Texas. What makes that game memorable?

A In the third inning, Nolan Ryan hit Chicago's Robin Ventura with a fastball. Ventura dropped his bat and charged the mound. Big mistake! Ryan, despite being 46 years old, lassoed Ventura with his left arm and started whacking on Ventura's noggin. The White Sox' third baseman was suspended for two games but not Ryan. He won both the fight and the game, with this stat line: 7 innings pitched, 5 strikeouts, 3 hits allowed, and 6 punches delivered.

Q What was the headline in the *Dallas Morning News'* sports section the next day?

A "Ryan throws six-hitter."

Q Carlton Fisk, an aloof New Englander, had skirmished with White Sox management almost from the moment he joined the club. His tenure ended badly—how so?

A By the early 1990s, he had begun to yield playing time to Ron Karkovice. He played only 25 games in 1993 as age finally took hold. Less than a week after he broke Bob Boone's record for most games caught, Fisk was released by the Sox. He was barred from joining his teammates in the clubhouse when they reached the playoffs. For this and other reasons, when he was elected to the Hall of Fame in 2000, Fisk announced that the sculpture forming his likeness would feature a Red Sox cap.

Q Jerry Reinsdorf bought the Chicago Bulls in 1985, so it only made sense that when Michael Jordan "retired" from basketball in 1994 to go into baseball, this was the organization he would sign with. Did the greatest hoopster of all time ever reach the big leagues?

A Not even close. He was assigned to the Sox' AA affiliate, the Birmingham Barons. Jordan, whose popularity helped shatter the club's season attendance record, batted .202, hit 3 homers, drove in 51 runs, and stole 30 bases. The Barons were probably the most publicized minor league team in the history of the game, with journalists from around the world on hand watching Jordan's progress, or lack thereof. Realizing the futility of his quest after one year, he went back to the hardcourts of the NBA.

Q Who were the "Mock Sox"?

A Chicago's would-be replacement team, recruited as a result of the 1994 major league players' strike. Like other franchises, the Sox put together a roster of scrubs, minor leaguers, and ex-major leaguers. They included Al Chambers, Dennis "Oil Can" Boyd, and a 37-year-old free agent pitcher named Ed Koziol, who hadn't pitched professionally in 16 years—and even that was in the low minors. Koziol never got a chance to pitch in the big leagues or a reasonable facsimile thereof. All plans to field replacement teams were dropped when the strike ended late in spring training of 1995.

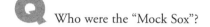

Q Where were the White Sox in the AL Central standings on August 11, 1994?

A They were on top (with a record of 67-46), one game ahead of the Cleveland Indians, when the season ended prematurely due to the players' strike.

Q Einhorn is also a top executive with the Chicago Bulls, so the names Reinsdorf and Einhorn have been fairly constant fixtures in the media for a quarter century now. Where did these two men attend law school?

A Northwestern University, just outside Chicago. Einhorn was selling hot dogs at Comiskey Park during the 1959 World Series.

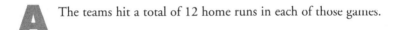

Q The White Sox and Tigers combined to set a major league record on May 18, 1995, and they matched it on July 2, 2002. What was the record?

A The teams hit a total of 12 home runs in each of those games.

Q When was Tim Raines' AL record of 40 straight stolen bases brought to a halt?

A On September 2, 1995, in a 10-4 defeat of Toronto.

Q What White Sox catcher had his season cut short when he was involved in a major home plate collision with the Royals' Johnny Damon on July 19, 1996?

A Chad Kreuter.

124

Q Although Ken Harrelson is regarded as a highly opinionated person, he is also one of the ultimate "homer" broadcasters, eschewing any pretense of objectivity. From the broadcast booth, he has coined many nicknames for popular Sox players. What are a few?

A Carlos "El Caballo" Lee, "Black Jack" McDowell, Frank "Big Hurt" Thomas, Craig "Little Hurt" Grebeck, Sammy "the Panther" Sosa, Lance "One-Dog" Johnson, and Herbert "the Milkman" Perry. Some of the names stuck, and others did not.

Q What was the earliest Opening Day in White Sox history?

A On March 31, 1996, Chicago fell to Seattle, 3-2, in 12 innings before a crowd of 57,467 at the Kingdome. Randy Johnson had 14 strikeouts for the Mariners.

Q The White Sox were the fourth of six teams in an 18-year career for switch-hitting Tony Phillips. They signed him as a free agent in 1996. How did he do that year?

A Phillips had one of the most productive seasons ever by a White Sox leadoff hitter. He led the league with 125 walks while posting a .404 on-base percentage. The feisty Phillips also showed some nice glove work, leading AL left fielders with 345 chances, 13 assists, and three double plays.

Q When did the Cubs and White Sox first meet in regular-season play?

A They had a three-game series at Comiskey Park in June 1997. The Cubbies won the opener, 8-3, but the White Sox bounced back to win the next two, 5-3 and 3-0.

Q The White Sox signed pitcher Jaime Navarro to a $5 million contract in 1997. Did they get their money's worth?

A His record was 9-14, he led the league in most earned runs allowed, hits allowed, and wild pitches, so evidently they did not. Navarro was even worse in '98 and was soon traded to the Brewers.

Q Who made an over-the-wall catch to rob Roberto Kelly of a two-run homer in the White Sox' 6-4 win at Minnesota in 1997?

A Mike Cameron.

Q Who were the three best-paid players on the 2003 White Sox roster?

A Outfielders Carl Everett ($9.15 million), Magglio Ordonez ($9 million), and pitcher Bartolo Colon ($8.25 million).

Q This outfielder, noted for his combative personality and disdain for the media, had eight very good years with the Cleveland Indians before signing a five-year, $55-million deal with the White Sox in 1997. Who was he?

A Albert Belle, whose splendid 1998 season included 49 home runs and 48 doubles. He invoked a clause in his contract that made him a free agent and was off to Baltimore for two more years before an arthritic hip ended his career. Belle, who finished with a .295 average and 381 homers, might have won a couple of MVP awards if not for his well-earned reputation for surliness.

Q What were a few of Belle's antisocial episodes?

A This man, who drew unflattering comparisons with ex-heavyweight champion and ex-con Sonny Liston, had a lot of them. He once threw a baseball at a fan who taunted him about his drinking problem. During the 1995 World Series, while with the Indians, he cursed—and then chased—a female reporter from the dugout. Some kids who had egged his condo nearly got run over by an enraged Belle in his car. His time in Chicago was turbulent, too. In 1997, he smashed the thermostat in the White Sox' locker room after a teammate had adjusted it. He spent a Kids' Day autograph session at the stadium reading the newspaper in the clubhouse; perhaps he was upset because of recent reports that he had lost $40,000 gambling on sports. Belle cursed a reporter whose only crime was standing along the cage during batting practice. In 1998, he was accused of domestic battery. When he went to Baltimore, it was more non-stop acrimony with team-mates, media, and fans.

What, in ChiSox history, was the "white flag" trade?

On July 31, 1997, the White Sox were 3½ games behind Cleveland—very much in the race for the AL Central title—at the trading deadline. General manager Ron Schueler, taking orders from owner Jerry Reinsdorf, unloaded rather than added veteran talent, sending Wilson Alvarez and Danny Darwin to San Francisco for five minor leaguers. The fire sale outraged fans and shocked the players. "I didn't know the season ended on August 1," said a glum Robin Ventura. Reinsdorf, still blamed by some for his role in the labor negotiations that led to the 1994 strike, was widely vilified. Home attendance dropped from 1.87 million in 1997 to 1.39 million two years later. Schueler and Reinsdorf soon found vindication, however. Four of the five youngsters who came over from the Giants contributed to the team winning 95 games and winning the division in 2000.

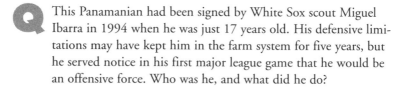

This Panamanian had been signed by White Sox scout Miguel Ibarra in 1994 when he was just 17 years old. His defensive limitations may have kept him in the farm system for five years, but he served notice in his first major league game that he would be an offensive force. Who was he, and what did he do?

Carlos Lee is the man, and on May 7, 1999, he became the first player in franchise history to homer in his first big league at-bat, victimizing Tom Candiotti of the A's at Comiskey Park. Lee was a regular in the Sox' lineup through the 2004 season. That December, "El Caballo" was dealt to Milwaukee for outfielder Scott Podsednik and pitcher Luis Vizcaino in a trade that played a major role in Chicago winning the 2005 World Series.

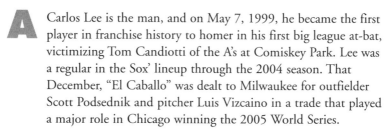

Q What was new with spring training for the White Sox in 1998?

A They switched from Florida ("the Grapefruit League"), their home for 44 years, to Arizona ("the Cactus League").

Q What rookie became the fourth player in White Sox history to hit for the cycle, achieving that feat on July 6, 1999?

A Chris Singleton did it in an 8-7 loss to the Kansas City Royals. Singleton singled in the first, tripled in the fourth, doubled in the fifth, and hit a home run in the seventh. His predecessors were Ray Schalk, Jack Brohamer, and Carlton Fisk.

Q In 2000, the White Sox sent pitchers Jaime Navarro and John Snyder to Milwaukee for pitcher Cal Eldred and shortstop Jose Valentin. Was it a wise move?

A Yes. Valentin and Eldred would be key players in the White Sox' run to the 2000 American League Central title, while Navarro and Snyder did little with the Brewers. Eldred was a surprising 10-2 with a 4.58 ERA for the '00 Sox before arm woes basically ended his season in midsummer. Valentin was not a great defensive player, but he would become the most prolific home-run-hitting shortstop in White Sox history. He hit at least 25 home runs in each of his five years in Chicago. Neither Appling, Carrasquel, nor Aparicio ever approached those numbers.

Q This pitcher, whose 100 saves is third best in team annals, was a key figure for the 2000 Central Division champs. In that season, he went 3-1 with a 2.97 ERA, saved 34 games, gave up just 66 hits, and struck out 91 in 88 innings. Name him.

A Keith Foulke.

Q After winning the 2000 AL Central title, the White Sox gave manager Jerry Manuel a contract extension through '04 with an option for '05. Would he last the contract?

A No. He was let go after the 2003 campaign and succeeded by Ozzie Guillen. But Manuel had enjoyed a good run. Besides that division crown, his teams finished second four times and third once. With exactly 500 wins, Manuel ranks fourth in club history.

Q On September 3, 2001, Chicago lost to Cleveland, 6-3. What player achieved a major career milestone that day?

A Designated hitter Jose Canseco stole the 200th base of his career, becoming just the ninth player in history to have that many steals and 400 home runs. Canseco, of course, will be remembered much longer for having blown the whistle on steroid abuse in major league baseball.

Q How much did Shoeless Joe Jackson's bat, "Black Betsy," sell for at an auction in 2001?

A $500,000.

Q In 2001, GM Kenny Williams was determined to land a No. 1 starter. Who did he get, and did it work out?

A He acquired 20-game winner David Wells from the Toronto Blue Jays in a five-player deal. And no, it did not work out. Wells spent an injury-shortened and disruptive year with the White Sox, going 5-7 with a 4.47 ERA.

Q The White Sox and Royals were playing a night game at New Comiskey Park in September 2002 when a rather shocking event took place. What was it?

A A 34-year-old father and his 15-year-old son came out of the stands and attacked Royals first base coach Tom Gamboa. Security was tightened at the stadium, but an almost identical incident happened there seven months later. It, too, involved a game against Kansas City; in this case, first base umpire Laz Diaz was tackled from behind by another boozed-up fan.

Q This third baseman spent a decade with the White Sox, then six years evenly divided among the Mets, Yankees, and Dodgers. He won six Gold Gloves and had 294 dingers—18 of which were grand slams. Identify him.

A Robin Ventura. Some baseball historians would say he was the greatest third baseman of the 1990s. Ventura, despite that ill-advised charge of Nolan Ryan in '93, is remembered for keeping an even keel and setting a good example for his teammates. He was a leader on every team for which he played.

Q The White Sox signed free agent pitcher Tom "Flash" Gordon to a one-year contract in 2003. How did the veteran right-hander with the knee-buckling curve do in that one year in Chicago?

A He wound up with a team-leading 12 saves, allowed just 57 hits in 74 innings, and struck out 91 batters.

Q What changed with Chicago's 12-year-old stadium in 2003?

A The White Sox forged a naming-rights agreement with U.S. Cellular, a Chicago-based wireless service provider, which was to pay the club $68 million over 20 years. A franchise press release held that the decision to change the name of the stadium from New Comiskey Park to U.S. Cellular Field was made to "pursue dramatic, fan-focused renovations and improvements to the ballpark." The money from the deal did, in fact, help to transform what had been a fairly cold edifice mocked by some as the "Mallpark" to a more classic, fan-friendly facility.

Q The White Sox gave free agent pitcher Esteban Loaiza a non-roster invitation to spring training in 2003. How did it go for this native of Mexico?

A Loaiza beat out several players and then proceeded to have an excellent season. He went 21-9 with a 2.90 ERA and led the AL with 207 strikeouts. Loaiza was the starting pitcher in the All-Star Game at U.S. Cellular Field and finished second in Cy Young voting.

Q Roberto Alomar played for 17 years, including the 2003 and '04 seasons with the White Sox. Some baseball historians regard him as one of the best second basemen ever (10 Gold Gloves, 12 All-Star appearances), but his career is overshadowed by what foul and noxious incident?

A On September 27, 1996, Alomar, while playing for Baltimore against Toronto, got into a heated argument over a called third strike with umpire John Hirschbeck and spat in his face. He was suspended for five games and fined $50,000. The notoriety Alomar brought upon himself from that event continues to linger.

Q How did the White Sox do against the Royals in Kansas City on September 27, 2003?

A Carl Everett and Joe Crede both had four RBIs, and Bartolo Colon snagged his 100th career win as Chicago enjoyed a 19-3 rout. The Sox had a season-high 21 hits, including seven doubles but no home runs.

Q On September 13 and 14, 2004, a couple of major league games were held at U.S. Cellular Field, but they did not involve the White Sox. So who played?

A The Florida Marlins and Montreal Expos. The series was supposed to have been played in south Florida, but Hurricane Ivan intervened. It was the first time a National League game had been played in an American League park since 1946. The two games drew fewer than 10,000 fans.

133

For 13 seasons, Ozzie Guillen was the Sox's light-hitting but quick-handed shortstop. He served as the team's manager when they won the World Series in 2005.

CHAPTER SIX

DEMONS EXORCISED

Chicago entered the 2005 season with a revamped and unproven lineup. But the doubters soon turned into believers as the White Sox built a 15-game lead in the American League Central. The Cleveland Indians narrowed it to 1½ before Ozzie Guillen's club rose to the occasion down the stretch with a 99-63 record. The best starting pitching in the league and a solid bullpen made the difference. But Chicago needed postseason success. In recent memory, the Sox had fallen short on three other occasions. In 1983, they lost three out of four games to the Baltimore Orioles. In 1993, the Toronto Blue Jays won in six. And in 2000, they were swept by the Seattle Mariners. Chicago lost in the first round of the playoffs each time.

In the early years of the new century, parity and unpredictability were the norm, as some of the top teams did pratfalls and perennial no-shows actually had a chance to grab the brass ring. In 2004, the Boston Red Sox, their large payroll notwithstanding, had won the World Series and ended eight decades of frustration and angst. If the BoSox, why not the ChiSox? They swept the defending champion Red Sox in the ALDS and moved on to defeat the Los Angeles Angels in five to take the American League pennant.

So there they were, back in the World Series for the first time since 1959—which Al Lopez' club had lost in six games to the Los Angeles Dodgers. Forty-six years between appearances was the longest in AL history. Returning to the Fall Classic meant a chance to emancipate Shoeless Joe and his infamous Black Sox.

Their opponents, the Houston Astros, also had a history of losing and close calls. After 42 years of existence, the Astros had beaten the Atlanta Braves and the defending NL champion St. Louis Cardinals to punch a ticket to the World Series. Houston fans could point to a hometown hero in 43-year-old Roger Clemens as proof that their time had come. Most baseball analysts predicted that the Astros would bring the title to the Lone Star State. Instead, the Sox got out the broom. Game 4 ended when shortstop Juan Uribe fielded a broken-bat grounder by Houston's Orlando Palmeiro and threw to first baseman Paul Konerko. Generations of people from all walks of life had a jubilant celebration in Chicago, especially on the South Side; most shocking of all, some Cubs fans admitted to cheering on the Sox.

Q How did the White Sox do in '04, when the Red Sox were en route to winning it all?

A They finished nine games behind Minnesota in the AL Central. Six teams in the league had better records.

Q He stands 6' 3", weighs 280 pounds, and his fastball comes in at 101 miles per hour. During his time in the Angels organization, he had elbow trouble and "off-field issues." The White Sox claimed him off waivers for $20,000, sent him to Birmingham, and then brought him up in July 2005. Who is this California native?

A Bobby Jenks, who appeared in every game of the 2005 World Series, pitching a total of five innings, and making the Series' final pitch. He had much success in 2006, converting 41 out of 45 save opportunities, with 80 K's. Jenks was selected to the All-Star Game in 2006 and 2007.

Q What does *Forbes* magazine estimate the value of the Chicago White Sox franchise at today?

A $300 million.

Q Despite Esteban Loaiza's 2003 performance, the Sox soon dealt him to the Yankees. What did they get in return?

A Jose Contreras, a big Cuban righty who was up and down through the first half of 2005 and then became one of the team's most reliable pitchers. He won his last eight starts and halted a couple of losing streaks. Contreras would also win three games in the post-season, including Game 1 of the World Series. Because he had defected from Cuba a few years earlier, Contreras' name was banned from being mentioned on Cuban TV, on orders from President Fidel Castro.

Q This speedy left fielder spent seven years toiling in the minor leagues, finished second in 2003 rookie of the year voting while with the Brewers, and came to the Sox in one of Kenny Williams' shrewd trades. Identify him. Hint: He is married to former Playboy playmate Lisa Dergan.

A Scott Podsednik. In 2005, he was a catalyst on a Chicago team that won its first World Series title since 1917. Although Podsednik spent time on the injured list, he stole a lot of bases, batted .290, and led the AL in infield hits. He quickly became a huge fan favorite at U.S. Cellular Field.

Q What second baseman did the Sox get from the Japanese Pacific League in 2005?

A Tadahito Iguchi, whose signing turned out to be one of GM Kenny Williams' best. Iguchi batted .278, hit 15 home runs, and drove in 71 runs for the '05 Pale Hose. His steady play greatly aided the team's charge to the World Series. Iguchi's three-run homer off David Wells of the Red Sox was the key hit in Game 2.

Q What free agent catcher did Chicago sign before the 2005 season?

A A.J. Pierzynski, who had a reputation as a clubhouse cancer in Minnesota and San Francisco. But he would prove to be a unifying force, hitting .257 with a career-high 18 home runs and 56 RBIs for the 2005 World Series champs. In the ALDS, Pierzynski hit .444 with two home runs and four RBIs as the Sox swept Boston. He homered in the five-game win over the Angels in the ALCS and continued his superb play against the Astros in the World Series. Pierzynski's performance would earn him the admiration of the Sox fan base, which had not been overly fond of him during his years with the Twins.

Q What unusual play involved Pierzynski in Game 2 of the 2005 AL championship series against the Los Angeles Angels?

A The score was tied with two out in the bottom of the ninth. Pierzynski was at the plate, with two strikes on him. He swung at a low pitch from the Angels' Kelvim Escobar and missed, for an apparent strike three. Catcher Josh Paul rolled the ball to the mound and headed to the dugout. Pierzynski, being a catcher, realized the umpire had not called him out, so he ran to first base (this is known as the "uncaught strike" rule). Pierzynski was safe at first. Pablo Ozuna, a pinch runner, replaced him and stole second base. Joe Crede drove him in three pitches later for a big post-season victory.

Q What players have been hit by the most pitches during their White Sox career?

A Minnie Minoso (145), Nellie Fox (125), Sherman Lollar (101), Carlton Fisk (84), and Frank Thomas (71).

Q Which White Sox pitchers have given up the most home runs?

A Billy Pierce (241), Ted Lyons (223), and Wilbur Wood (193).

Q Who are Chicago's all-time strikeout leaders?

A Billy Pierce (1,796), Ed Walsh (1,732), Red Faber (1,471), Wood (1,332), and Gary Peters (1,098).

Q And which batters have whiffed the most?

A Frank Thomas (1,165), Harold Baines (918), Fisk (798), Ray Durham (758), and Ron Karkovice (749).

Q Who are the leaders in stolen bases?

A Eddie Collins (368), Luis Aparicio (318), Frank Isbell (250), Lance Johnson (226), and Ray Durham (219).

Q Which Sox have hit the most triples?

A Shano Collins and Fox are tied with 104. Next on the list are Luke Appling and Eddie Collins (102 each), and Johnny Mostil (82).

Q Which Sox have come to the plate most?

A Luke Appling (10,243), Nellie Fox (9,446), Frank Thomas (8,602), Eddie Collins (7,405), and Harold Baines (6,797).

Q Who are the franchise leaders in hits?

A Luke Appling (2,749), Nellie Fox (2,470), Frank Thomas (2,136), Eddie Collins (2,007), and Harold Baines (1,773).

Q Who have made the most errors?

A Luke Appling (672), Buck Weaver (395), Lee Tannehill (313), George Davis (258), and Eddie Collins (246).

Q Who are Chicago's leaders in batting average?

A Joe Jackson (.340), Eddie Collins (.331), Zeke Bonura (.317), Bibb Falk (.315), and Taffy Wright (.312).

Q Who have thrown the most wild pitches?

A Ed Walsh (75), Tommy John (67), Joel Horlen and Gary Peters (64 each), and Wilbur Wood (63).

Q What ChiSox pitchers have won the most games?

A Ted Lyons (260), Red Faber (260), Ed Walsh (195), Billy Pierce (186), and Wilbur Wood (163).

Q Where could most of the White Sox be found on February 13, 2006?

A The World Series champion White Sox were honored in a ceremony at the White House. President George W. Bush was there, but not manager Ozzie Guillen, who said he was on vacation. Jermaine Dye and Paul Konerko presented Bush—formerly the owner of the Texas Rangers—with a White Sox jacket. The president, in a jocular mood, recognized several players in a meeting that lasted about 11 minutes.

Q On May 20, 2006, the Cubs and White Sox added a new chapter to a rivalry full of mutual loathing. What happened?

A In a game at U.S. Cellular Field, catcher A.J. Pierzynski and his counterpart with the Cubs, Michael Barrett, brawled in the bottom of the second inning. The two teams joined in with enthusiasm, and four men were ejected. When play resumed, Scott Podsednik quickly got on, loading the bases, and second baseman Tadahito Iguchi busted a grand-slam home run to send the White Sox to a 7-0 win. Quite naturally, Chicago sports radio and the Internet chat rooms were hopping that night.

Q How did the 2006 White Sox rank in terms of salary figures?

A The players' payroll was about $103 million, trailing the Yankees ($198 million), Red Sox ($120 million), and Angels ($104 million). At the bottom were the Florida Marlins ($15 million).

Q April 18, 2007, was a good night for the Sox. What happened at U.S. Cellular Field?

A Mark Buehrle threw a no-hitter against Texas. He struck out eight while allowing one walk in the 6-0 victory. The 28-year-old Buehrle used a nasty mix of offspeed stuff and high heat in beating the Rangers. He was complemented by a grand slam by Jermaine Dye and a couple of one-run shots by Jim Thome, plus key defensive plays by shortstop Juan Uribe, third baseman Joe Crede, and second baseman Tadahito Iguchi. It was the 16th no-hitter in team history. Buehrle's comment: "I can't believe I did it. Perfect game would have been nice, too."

Q Sixteen years passed between Wilson Alvarez's no-hitter against Baltimore in 1991 and that of Buehrle against Texas in 2007. Have the Sox ever had a longer gap between no-nos?

A Yes. Bill Dietrich threw one against St. Louis in 1937, and 20 years passed before Bob Keegan had his against Washington.

Q What is the Chicago Transit Authority's Red Line?

A It is a commuter train running north-south through the Windy City's neighborhoods, stopping at U.S. Cellular Field and Wrigley Field. It is sometimes said that this is the only thing the White Sox and Cubs have in common.

Q The 2007 White Sox were 13 games behind Detroit at the All-Star break. What had gone wrong for a team that ruled baseball less than two years earlier?

A There were major offensive meltdowns by veterans like Paul Konerko, Jermaine Dye, and Tadahito Iguchi. Several power pitchers in the bullpen (such as Mike MacDougal and David Aardsma) were so bad as to get demoted to the minors. And manager Ozzie Guillen sounded like he might not be around too much longer, voluntarily or otherwise.

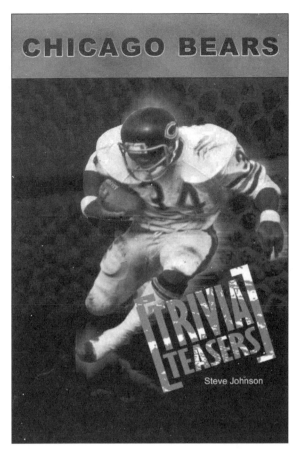

Chicago Bears Trivia Teasers

Steve Johnson

The Bears are back! Now you can "bear down" with more than 400 brainteasers about one of the oldest and winningest teams in the NFL. From Papa Bear and the Staleys though the Super Bowl '80s to today, this book will make you "da expert."

Softcover / 5.5 x 8.5 / 152 pages / List $16.96
ISBN 13: 978-1-931599-76-4

For these and other great Trails Books titles,
call (800) 258-5830 or visit us online at www.trailsbooks.com

Chicago Cubs Trivia Teasers
Steve Johnson

Think you're a real Cubbies fan? Test your knowledge against more than 400 trivia questions that cover the entire history of the most storied team in baseball. Holy cow!

Softcover / 5.5 x 8.5 / 152 pages / List $16.96
ISBN 13: 978-1-931599-75-7

**For these and other great Trails Books titles,
call (800) 258-5830 or visit us online at www.trailsbooks.com**